C000200978

LITTLE BOOK OF THE

WORLD CUP

LITTLE BOOK OF THE

WORLD CUP

First published in the UK in 2005

© G2 Entertainment Limited 2014

www.G2ent.co.uk

Printed and bound in Europe

ISBN 978-1-909040-01-4

Contents

Alberto

Born in Rio De Janeiro on 17 July 1944, Carlos Alberto Torres began his professional career with the Fluminense club of Rio De Janeiro at the age of 19. In 1966 he linked up with Pelé at Santos FC, remaining with the club for eight years. This period saw his greatest achievements as a player, culminating in captaining the brilliant Brazilian side to victory in the 1970 World Cup in Mexico. Carlos Alberto not only had the honour of holding the trophy aloft, which Brazil had won outright, he also scored the Final goal in the 4-1 victory over Italy, racing up from his full-back position to smash an unstoppable drive home. As such he is considered the template for the likes of Roberto Carlos and Cafu. Carlos returned to Fluminense in 1974, going on to help the club win back to-back Carioca League championships.

In 1977 he moved to rivals Flamengo, but before the year was out had headed to the north of the continent, linking once again with Pelé at New York Cosmos. He won two consecutive titles, in 1977 and 1978, before moving across the country to join California Surf but returned to Cosmos in 1982, where he won his final League championship in the same year before his retirement as a player. Carlos then moved into management, a role that has seen him in charge of the Nigerian, Oman and Azerbaijan national sides as well as club roles in Brazil, the United States and Egypt. However, the Azerbaijanis' failure to progress in the World Cup qualifiers saw him on the job market in 2005. Later that year, he insulted the referee and blamed his team's relegation on a conspiracy when in charge of Brazilian club side Paysandu.

Argentina

Argentina has an illustrious World Cup history, winning the trophy twice, although results in recent years have been a disappointment to the country's fanatical fans. The first World Cup, held in 1930, saw them defeat France, Mexico, Chile and the USA on their way to the Final, scoring an aggregate of 16 goals to their opponents' four.

They failed at the last hurdle, however, going down 4-2 to Uruguay. They reached the Final stages in 1934, 1958, 1962 and 1966, but Argentina's only notable achievement during this long period was their quarter-final appearance in 1966 when they lost to England via a Geoff Hurst goal and had captain Rattin sent off. In 1974 they reached the Group A quarter-final stage, where they lost to Holland (4-0) and Brazil (2-1) before scraping a 1-1 draw with East Germany.

In 1978 it was to be very different. The World Cup finals were held in Argentina, even though many felt the unstable political situation might lead to security problems. Although the home nation lost a Group 1 game to Italy, they

beat Hungary and France to progress to the Group B quarterfinals. There, Argentina defeated Poland and Peru, and drew with Brazil. It was enough to see them through to the Final, where they met Holland and, after extra time, ran out 3-1 winners, including a double from Mario Kempes.

Argentina achieved little in 1982, but four years later they again won the trophy. Having progressed to the quarter-finals in Mexico, they faced England and won in controversial circumstances.

Maradona put two past Peter Shilton, one way or another, and Gary Lineker's goal proved insufficient to keep England in the competition. In the semi-final, Argentina beat Belgium 2-0, Maradona again scoring the goals, and then they defeated West Germany 3-2 in the Final. For once, every England supporter was supporting Germany. Since 1986 it has been downhill all the way – although Argentina did reach the Final again in 1990. This time, West Germany took their revenge, running out 1-0 winners. In 1994 Argentina came nowhere, and in 1998 they were beaten 2-1 by Holland in the quarterfinals.

In 2002 they went out in disastrous fashion in the group stages and although they improved in 2006 they eventually went out in the quarter-finals to Germany 4-2 on penalties. However, hope sprung in 2010 when Maradona took over. Despite topping their group with three wins and a second round win over Mexico, their 4-0 drubbing to Germany in the last eight gave Maradona's critics fresh ammunition over his poor tenure, which included a tempestuous qualification campaign.

Banks

Born in 1937, Gordon Banks began his career at Chesterfield and then played for Leicester City and Stoke. He made his full international debut in 1963. A goalkeeper of exceptional quality, with amazing powers of concentration and an unrivalled technique, he was to play for his country 73 times, concede 57 goals, and keep a remarkable 35 clean sheets. The 1966 World Cup was the highlight of his career. Banks conceded just three goals in six games, his remarkable agility contributing greatly towards the famous 4-2 victory over Germany in the Final.

The 1970 World Cup saw a brilliant performance in a group game against Brazil. Banks made a miraculous one-handed save, tipping a fearsome, bouncing header from Pelé over the bar.

England lost 1-0, but Banks had kept a clean sheet in a 1-0 win over Romania and went on to record another in a 1-0 win over Czechoslovakia, thus ensuring England qualified for a quarterfinal against West Germany. Sadly, he reported sick for that match – there were rumours that he had been poisoned – and England went out of the competition. Banks' career ended in 1972 when a car crash cost him the sight of one eye. He was perhaps England's greatest ever 'keeper.

Above: *Banks makes a remarkable save from a header by Pelé during their first round match in the 1970 World Cup*

Baresi

An elegant sweeper, Franco Baresi was the defensive linchpin of the all-conquering Macmillan side of the late 1980s and early 1990s but had to bide his time before bringing his talents onto the world stage. Baresi's flawless reading of the game, terrific positional sense and great composure meant he was a huge favourite in Italy, where the beauty of defending has long been appreciated. His ability to bring the ball out from the back and help to create attacking options was revolutionary. However, Italian national manager Enzo Bearzot, in charge for the 1982 World Cup squad, left him on the bench as Italy lifted the cup.

Baresi decided to opt out of playing for his country while Bearzot was in charge so did not make his World Cup bow until 1990, when Italy lost on penalties to Argentina at the semi-final stage. Four years on Baresi, now 34, was captain when Italy travelled to America. It was an incident-packed tournament for the AC Milan stalwart – he underwent knee surgery in the middle of the competition but returned to play with typical aplomb in the goal-less Final against Brazil. There was no happy ending, though, as he was one of two Italians to miss a spot-kick and Brazil won the shoot-out 3-2.

Battles

In the 1938 world cup Brazil faced Czechoslovakia in Bordeaux. The Final scoreline was 1-1 but the more pertinent statistics were two broken limbs, a bad stomach injury and three dismissals. Brazil were again involved in 1954 in the Battle of Berne. Hungary were 2-0 ahead in the quarter-final clash when Brazil netted a penalty and the contest became progressively more violent. Brazil's Nilton Santos and Hungarian captain József Bozsik were sent off after a punch-up and Brazil's Humberto Tozzi followed them for kicking Lorant. Hungary won 4-2 but post-match brawls brought further disgrace to the competition.

However, even that was tame compared to the infamous Battle of Santiago between Chile and Italy in 1962. Prior to a BBC highlights programme, David Coleman introduced the Group B encounter with the words: "The game you are about to see is the most stupid, appalling, disgusting and disgraceful exhibition of football." The first foul came after a mere 12 seconds and the first dismissal after just eight minutes –

although Giorgio Ferrini refused to leave and had to be dragged off, kicking and screaming, by policemen. It took almost 10 minutes before play, and the violence, continued. Chilean Leonel Sanchez reacted to a series of kicks from Mario David by flattening him; David responded by kicking Sanchez in the neck and was sent off. Almost lost in the mayhem was that Italy's nine men lost 2-0.

Right:
*Beckenbauer was
the first captain to
lift the new FIFA
trophy, 1974*

Below: *World Cup
winning Manager
Beckenbauer*

Beckenbauer

Franz Beckenbauer is the only man to have won the World Cup both as captain and manager. However, he is recognised not for the stack of silverware gleaned over a long and distinguished career in football, but for his style and genius. He was the master of the sweeper's position, and achieved legendary status by operating as an attacking defensive player, and doing so with an air of arrogance that earned his the nicknames 'Emperor Franz' and 'The Kaiser'.

Beckenbauer kicked off his World Cup career in 1966, a tournament that culminated in England's famous 4-2 victory over West Germany at Wembley. Four years later in Mexico the West Germans had their revenge, with Beckenbauer scoring the goal that started his side's revival against England in the quarter-finals. The Germans eventually claimed third spot with a win over Uruguay, although the lasting memory of Beckenbauer was in the classic 4-3 semi-final defeat to Italy in which he'd played with a heavily strapped shoulder.

The Kaiser captained his country to glory in Munich in 1974, meaning he now had the complete set of World Cup medals: gold, silver and bronze. But he was far from finished with the World Cup. After taking over the German national team hotseat in 1984 he guided his country to the Final in 1986 and then, via a dramatic semi-final penalty shoot-out victory against England, to the Cup in 1990.

Beckham

David Beckham became both hero and villain in the 1998 World Cup. Something of a schoolboy prodigy, he joined Manchester United at an early age, and went on to become a midfield icon. As well as perfect crosses, he soon established himself in the England side, first becoming its captain during the 2000-01 season, and was famed for his accurate and rocket-like free kicks.

In 1998 Beckham made his World Cup mark by scoring with a stunning free-kick against Colombia. Then, against Argentina, he was sent off for kicking out at Diego Simeone and became, for a while, a national villain. It was the first red card of his career, and England lost the game. The press, so adept at building players up to knock them down again, had a field day, but Beckham learned from his mistake.

In October 2001 his last-gasp goal against Greece ensured England qualified for the 2002 finals, although a broken bone in his foot meant he was not fully fit for much of that tournament. Following England's disappointing defeat at the hands of Portugal in the 2006 tournament he

decided to step down as Captain. Despite losing his squad place under McLaren he was rejuvenated under Fabio Capello and looked to be in contention for his fourth World Cup until a heartbreaking Achilles injury playing for Milan ended his hopes.

Above: *Beckham playing for AC Milan on his loan spell from LA Galaxy, which he hopes will become permanent*

Left: *Beckham taking his penalty kick against Argentina in 2002*

Brazil

The Brazilians have an unrivalled World Cup record, having won the trophy on five occasions. They showed the first signs of their eventual dominance in the 1950 competition, when they reached the Final on their native soil. Almost 200,000 people packed into the Maracana Stadium for a game against Uruguay. Due to the somewhat strange arrangements made for this first post-war World Cup competition, this was technically not the Final but a 'final pool' match. However, as Brazil had already beaten Sweden 7-1 and Spain 6-1, they needed only to draw with Uruguay to win the Cup. Sadly for most of the fans squashed into the Maracana they fell at the last hurdle, going down 2-1.

In 1954 Brazil reached only the quarter-final stage, but 1958 saw them win the cup for the first time. They beat France 5-2 in the semis, Pelé grabbing a hat-trick, and then beat hosts Sweden by the same score in the Final, Pelé scoring twice. Four years later, they retained the trophy in Chile, beating England 3-1 in the quarter-final, Chile 4-2 in the last four

and Czechoslovakia 3-1 in the Final.

In 1966 Brazil went out early, having been beaten 3-1 by both Hungary and Portugal but, normal service was resumed in Mexico in 1970. Brazil won all their group games, before beating Peru in the quarter-final and exacting belated revenge over Uruguay in the semis. Italy were duly dispatched in the Final 4-1.

For the next 20 years, Brazilian football rather lost its way, but in 1994 the team once more made it to a World Cup Final. Having disposed of Sweden with a single Romario goal, they took on an injury-stricken Italian side. The game failed to live up to expectations and finished 0-0, Romario heading wide from close range during extra time. Brazil then won 3-2 on penalties.

The boys from Brazil were back. Four years later they once more reached the Final, but this time they received a rare hammering, being beaten 3-0 by France. Undeterred, they returned with a vengeance in 2002 when they took the trophy for the fifth time by beating Germany 2-0. Ronaldo scored both goals in the second half. The German 'keeper Oliver Kahn was player of the tournament – but Brazil had won the World Cup. The 2006 and 2010 tournaments were not as successful, knocked out by France and the Dutch respectively in the quarter-finals.

Brothers

There have been a surprising number of siblings at World Cup finals over the years. The first Finals in 1930 saw brothers Manuel and Filipe Rosas and Rafael and Francisco Gutierrez star for Mexico, while Mario and Juan Evaristo went all the way to the Final with Uruguay. The first pair to win the trophy were Germans Fritz and Ottmar Walter. They each scored twice in the 6-1 semi-final drubbing of Austria before helping their side to a 3-2 win over favourites Hungary. The chalk and cheese Charlton brothers, Bobby and Jack, were ever-present for World Champions England in 1966. The most recent World Cup Final brothers were West Germans Karl-Heinz and Bernd Foerster in 1982, but they were unable to stop Italy winning 3-2.

The only twins to score at the World Cup finals were the Van de Kerkhofs, René andWilly who starred for Holland in 1978. Francois Omam-Biyik and André Kana-Biyik helped Cameroon become the first African side to reach the quarter-finals in 1990 while Michael and Brian Laudrup sparkled for Denmark in 1998. In that same tournament Tore Andre Flo and Jostein Flo played for Norway, along with cousin Havard Flo. Most unlucky World Cup siblings were probably Victor and Vyacheslav Chanov,

goalkeeping brothers who were named in Russia's 1982 squad but sat on the bench throughout, unable to displace the great Rinat Dassajev.

In 2010, the Boatengs became the first brothers to play against each other in the tournament; Jerome represented Germany, while brother Kevin-Prince played for Ghana. Honduras then became the first country to select three brothers in their squad after calling up Jerry Palacios, who joined brothers Wilson and Johnny in South Africa.

Above: *Brian Laudrup of Denmark with the ball during the quarter-final match against Brazil in 1998*

Left: *Danish captain Michael Laudrup grapples for the ball against Nigeria, 1998*

Cheats

Cheats never prosper, according to the famous saying, but many have tried over the years! Cheating comes in a variety of forms; taking prohibited drugs, diving to win a penalty, feigning injury or any other action designed to give one team or another an unfair advantage over their opponents. There is little doubt that the most blatant example of cheating involved not one player or one team but all 22 players who took part in the West Germany and Austria match in 1982. Both sides took to the field knowing exactly what they needed to do in order to progress out of the group stage – a 1-0 victory for the Germans would enable Germany and Austria to put out the Algerians.

And that is exactly how the match panned out – Germany took the lead after ten minutes and neither side showed any interest in making a proper game of it thereafter. The supposedly neutral Spanish crowd, egged on by a number of Algerians, whistled and jeered throughout. Even one or two

German fans were embarrassed, with one setting fire to his national flag, but the game ended a 1-0 win for Germany. Despite Algerian protestations to FIFA, the result was allowed to stand (although the match did result in a change in the timing of games, with the final group matches now taking place at exactly the same time) and Germany continued their progress towards the Final. The Germans benefited from another outrageous slice of fortune in the semi-final with goalkeeper Harald Schumacher unpunished for knocking out Patrick Battiston of France as he looked certain to score. If there was any justice, then it came in the Final where Italy put paid to the Germans 3-1. The opening goal came from Paolo Rossi, who had previously been barred for bribery.

Cole

If you can bypass Ashley Cole's off-field incidents, then many believe that the former Arsenal and current Chelsea player to be one of England's best left-backs of recent times.

He was instrumental in guiding Chelsea to Champions League glory in Munich in 2012, and will be an experienced head in Roy Hodgson's side at the 2014 World Cup – Cole's last.

Born on Dec 20 1980 in Stepney, Cole joined Arsenal as a teenager in 1998 and made his first-team debut at the age of 18 as a striker against Middlesbrough.

After a brief spell on loan at Crystal Palace in 2000, he cemented his position as Arsenal's left back when Brazilian Sylvinho suffered an injury later that year.

Two Premier League titles and three FA Cups ensued before he and his agent were caught in a secret meeting with Chelsea manager Jose Mourinho and chief executive Peter Kenyon in Jan 2005.

Yet, he is still a rare jewel as far as full-backs go in English football and has the ability to defend and attack in equal measure.

England have, of course, flattered to deceive on the international stage and Cole, like many of his teammates, have failed to deliver despite bringing success on the club stage. Winning over 100 caps for his country, Cole has also played more internationals without scoring – more than any other outfield player in England history.

Above: *Ashley Cole of England in action during the FIFA 2010 World Cup*

Cruyff

The extraordinarily gifted, hugely influential Johan Cruyff stands as the greatest ever Dutch player and one of the very best players of all time. Brilliant, yet outspoken, Cruyff guided Holland to the 1974 World Cup Final but had to settle for a runners-up medal as they were pipped by West Germany. A clash with the Dutch footballing authorities meant that he declined to play in the 1978 tournament. It was Cruyff 's club side, Ajax, then Holland who brought the concept of 'total football' to the world stage – and it was Cruyff 's vision, intelligence and supreme versatility that allowed it to work so effectively. Total football relies on players within the team to be capable of switching into each other's roles as circumstances dictate.

Within this highly technical framework Cruyff, the Dutch captain, pulled the strings and, although nominally a centre-forward, he popped up all over the park with devastating effect.

Famously he also brought us the 'Cruyff turn' – in a group match with Sweden he was seemingly going nowhere, tight against the touchline with a defender at close quarters. Cruyff shaped to cross but instead cleverly dragged the ball behind his standing leg and raced away leaving the hapless full-back running the wrong way. He won a hat-trick of European Cups with Ajax and was European Footballer of the Year three times. After a spell in the USA he turned to management, in which he was to prove equally innovative and successful at Ajax and Barcelona.

Czechoslovakia

Twice beaten Finalists, the break-up of the Czechoslovakian nation during the 1990s ensures that the name of Czechoslovakia will never get engraved on the World Cup. One of the many European countries that sat out the inaugural tournament in Uruguay in 1930, Czechoslovakia made their debut in Italy in 1934, going on to reach the Final before being beaten by Italy after extra time 2-1 despite having taken the lead.

Despite the threat of a different nature from Germany come 1938, Czechoslovakia lined up in France and won their opening match, beating Holland 3-0 after extra time. Extra time was also needed in their second match, against Brazil, but a 1-1 draw meant a replay, with Brazil going through 2-1.

After failing to get further than the group stage in 1958 Czechoslovakia produced their best performance in Chile in 1962. A hesitant start saw them qualify from a group that included Spain, Brazil and Mexico before beginning to find their form throughout the tournament. Victory over Hungary by 1-0 put them in the semi-final where they overwhelmed Yugoslavia 3-1 to make the Final and face holders and favourites Brazil. Brazil were in fact riding their luck, with Pelé out injured and Garrincha more than fortunate to have been given a reprieve and allowed to play despite having been sent off in the semi-final!

Masopust gave Czechoslovakia the lead after quarter of an hour, only for Brazil to equalise two minutes later. Two goals in the second half secured the title for Brazil and represented the peak of Czechoslovakia's World Cup exploits to date. They qualified for both the 1970 and 1982 Finals but were eliminated in the first stage, getting out of the group stage in 1990 only to be beaten 1-0 by eventual winners Germany in the quarter-final. Since the dissolution in 1993, the Czech Republic have only qualified for one World Cup, in 2006.

Denmark

Widely regarded as one of the strongest European nations, Denmark has yet to achieve any real impact on the World Cup. They did not even bother competing until 1958 and did not qualify for the finals until the 1986 tournament in Mexico. There they looked as though they could prove to be the surprise package, winning a group that included former World Champions West Germany and Uruguay with three straight victories.

It would be hard to pick between their 2-0 victory over the Germans and the 6-1 demolition of the Uruguayans as the ultimate performance, but certainly the world was paying close attention to a side that featured such stars as Morten Olsen, Michael Laudrup, Frank Arnesen, Allan Simonsen and Jan Molby. It all blew up in the second round, however, Spain winning 5-1 even though the Danes had taken the lead! Denmark then disappeared from view until 1998 when they reached France and once again qualified out of the group stages, albeit having stumbled to victory over Saudi Arabia, drawn with South Africa and lost narrowly to eventual winners France.

After overcoming the Nigerians 4-1 in the second round Denmark fell to the Brazilians 3-2 in the quarter-finals. They were drawn in with the French again in 2002, this time winning 2-0, their second victory in a group they topped ahead of Uruguay and Senegal, but England proved too strong in the second round by 3-0. However they have disappointed since, qualifying for the 2010 Finals, but missing out on Brazil.

Didi

While the 1958 World Cup became known as the tournament that first revealed the talents of Pelé to the world, there were plenty of other stars within the victorious Brazilian side, not least Didi. Born Valdir Pereira in Rio de Janeiro on 8 October 1929, Didi played his club football with Botafogo and Fluminense and was rated one of the best players to have represented either of these clubs.

His honours and awards within the game are almost without equal – he scored the very first goal at the Maracana stadium, made his Brazil debut in 1952 and went on to make 68 appearances over the next ten years, scoring 20 goals. It is his influence and his falling-leaf free-kicks that ensured his place in Brazilian folklore; after four minutes of the 1958 World Cup Final Brazil found themselves a goal down to the host nation Sweden and had yet to touch the ball. Didi gathered the ball from the net and as he made his way up towards the centre circle, deliberately spoke to each and every member of the Brazilian side to motivate them. Brazil equalised four minutes later and went on

to win 5-2 with a masterly performance.

Didi added a second winners' medal in 1962 in the 3-1 win over Czechoslovakia in what was his third final tournament and promptly bowed out from international football, as good a time to retire as any. That was not Didi's final appearance in the World Cup finals however, for in 1970 he guided Peru to the quarter-finals (the first time they had actually qualified) with a side reminiscent of the Brazilians in their reliance on attack as being the best form of defence. Peru finally lost to Brazil in the quarter-finals, but their 4-2 defeat was one of the best games of the tournament. Didi, the Master, died on 12 May 2001.

Dismissals

As is well known, the very first World Cup finals were held in Uruguay in 1930, where a number of firsts were recorded, including the first goal and the first hat-trick. Not to be outdone, the 1930 finals saw the first dismissal, Mario De Las Casas of Peru earning his marching orders in the group match against Romania. Four years later Markos of Hungary joined the Hall of Shame, dismissed in the second round match against Austria.

Since the first two tournaments, which saw two dismissals, a further 157 players have been sent off. It would be pointless trying to work out an average per tournament, for different rules and interpretations have been in use at various points, but there have nonetheless been some noteworthy moments. The third tournament, in France in 1938, saw four dismissals, three of which came in the Brazil and Czechoslovakia match, Machado and Zeze Procopio of Brazil joining Riha for an early bath during the 1-1 draw. Fortunately the replay passed without incident!

The tournament held in Brazil in 1950 was the first tournament where no one received their marching orders, but Brazil were once again on the receiving end in 1954; all three of the tournament's dismissals came in the notorious Battle of Berne between Brazil and Hungary, Santos and Tozzi of Brazil joining Bozsik in being sent off by Arthur Ellis. Brazil has the worst disciplinary record in the finals, having had nine players sent off (a tally that has been equalled by Argentina).

Brazil can at least claim that their expulsions have come in 17 tournaments; Cameroon has managed to have seven dismissals in just five finals. Three of these came in the 1998 tournament, where eventual champions France also suffered a trio of disciplinary lapses. Although red and yellow cards were first introduced at the 1970 tournament in Mexico, this was only the second finals where no-one was sent off, so the honour of being the first player to have a red card brandished at him goes to Chile's Caszely, sent off in the match against West Germany on 14 June 1974.

Cameroon's Rigobert Song is the only player to have been sent off twice, a feat achieved against Brazil in 1994 and Chile four years later.

Up until 1990, the standard of behaviour in the Final was such that no player had received his marching orders, but the match between holders Argentina and Germany (itself a repeat of the 1986 Final) changed all that, with Pedro Monzon of Argentina earning the dubious honour. He only just managed it, for later in the game teammate Gustavo Dezotti joined him in the dressing room before the match was over. The tournament in France 1998 was the worst as far as discipline is concerned, with 22 players receiving their marching orders. This tournament also saw the last appearance of Arturio Brizio Carter of Mexico, the most trigger happy of all referees – he sent

off seven players in the six games he was in charge of at the 1994 and 1998 finals!

Since Dezotti's dismissal, Marcel Desailly (1998), Zinedine Zidane (2006) and John Heitinga (2010) have all been sent off in a World Cup final.

Embarrassing Moments

World-class clangers are fortunately few and far between during the World Cup finals, but when they happen they are often earth-shattering. The 1966 World Cup in England is usually reckoned to have been a well-organised affair, but the tournament was not without incident; a special commemorative stamp produced by the Post Office and approved by the Football Association showing the flags of the 16 competing nations had to be withdrawn after the Foreign Office pointed out that the British Government did not recognise North Korea!

The opening match of the finals, where England drew 0-0 with Uruguay, was nearly abandoned even before it kicked off when the referee discovered that seven of the England players had forgotten their identity cards – a police outrider was dispatched to the hotel in order to collect them. At least the players could claim they had other things on their mind; the 1974 Final between West Germany and Holland was delayed after referee Jack Taylor noticed the corner and midfield flags were missing!

The 1974 World Cup also produced one of the biggest clangers of all time midway through the group match between Yugoslavia and Zaire in 1974. Widely reckoned to have been one of the less entertaining of all World Cups, we can at least thank Zaire defender N'daye for attempting to liven up matters. Yugoslavia were awarded a free kick just outside the Zaire penalty area, with Zaire lining up a solid-looking wall. The referee put his whistle to his mouth, gave a short blast to indicate that the free kick could be taken and was then horrified to see N'daye come racing out of the wall

and boot the ball into touch!

Not surprisingly, the referee took a dim view at this and promptly sent him off. At least N'daye managed to connect with the ball properly and project it to where he wanted – this seemingly simple task proved beyond one of the biggest stars in the world. It was a moment that will be forever etched on the minds of those who witnessed the opening ceremony of the 1994 World Cup in America, a ceremony that was planned down to the last detail. Singing superstar Diana Ross was to perform a specially written song and then,

towards the end, symbolically kick an oversize ball into a goal that would then collapse as Diana ran through the net. Diana performed the song well enough, ran among the children gathered on the field, took a swing at the ball, which was no more than five yards from the goal, and connected perfectly. Except, even from five yards, she missed the goal. Fortunately someone was on hand to pull the goal apart anyway. It was almost fate that the competition that began with a missed penalty by Diana Ross should end with one missed by Roberto Baggio.

England

Engand failed to take the World Cup seriously when it all began in 1930. This was partly due to the fact that they had left FIFA in 1928, following a dispute over payments to amateurs, but in truth they were simply not interested in this new-fangled and rather unnecessary competition. They got it wrong, of course, and, having missed out in 1934 and 1938 as well, England eventually deigned to participate in 1950.

The 1950 World Cup was to be held in Brazil, and most England players,

unless they had fought in the War, had not previously been much further than Blackpool. England started well enough, but then, astonishingly, lost 1-0 to the USA. They then lost to Spain and home they went.

By 1962, where they reached the last eight, the competition was being taken very seriously and it was clear that, if England were ever going to succeed, they would have no better chance than in 1966 – on home soil.

England started boringly enough, with a goalless draw against Uruguay in their first group game. They followed this up with 2-0 victories over Mexico and France, Bobby Charlton and Roger Hunt scoring in the first of these games, Hunt scoring both in the second. A 1-0

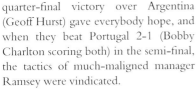

quarter-final victory over Argentina (Geoff Hurst) gave everybody hope, and when they beat Portugal 2-1 (Bobby Charlton scoring both) in the semi-final, the tactics of much-maligned manager Ramsey were vindicated.

The Final, against West Germany, was played at Wembley. The line-up was: Banks, Cohen, Wilson, Stiles, J. Charlton, Moore, Ball, Hunt, R. Charlton, Hurst and Peters. Germany scored after 13 minutes, but six minutes later Hurst headed an equaliser following a Bobby Moore free kick. On 78 minutes, Martin Peters scored what would surely be the winner, but the West Germans equalised from a disputed free-kick shortly before the final whistle. In extra time Hurst thumped a shot onto the underside of the crossbar, and the Russian linesman signalled a goal. That decision has been debated ever since, but the goal stood – and Hurst then added another. It was all over, and England had won the World Cup.

Time has not been kind ever since. There have been highs – England reaching the semi-finals at Italia '90 – but too many lows. The most recent of which came in 2010 when a blighted campaign finished acrimoniously against the Germans. With Germany leading Fabio Capello's side 2-1 in their second-round clash, a legitimate goal by England midfielder Frank Lampard was ruled not to have crossed the line when television replays clearly showed otherwise. Germany went on to win 4-1.

Above: *That elusive third goal struck by Geoff Hurst*

Right: *Andres Escobar during Colombia's 2-1 loss to the USA in the 1994 World Cup*

Escobar

Having lost to Romania in their opening group match of the 1994 World Cup, Colombia knew they had to beat the US in Pasadena to stay in the competition. It was a match that would have tragic consequences for defender Andres Escobar.

In his book The Story Of The World Cup Brian Glanville writes: "That the Colombians lay down and died now seems beyond all possible doubt. Why they did is another matter. Out of fear? Out of gambling greed? What we do know is that they were unrecognisable, even if the Americans needed an own goal from Andres Escobar, after 35 minutes, to go ahead."

The Colombian team was one of those expected to do well in the tournament but before the game had received death threats while Colombian drug cartels were widely thought to have been betting on the national team. The US went on to win 2-1 and the Colombians left the competition earlier than expected.

Days later, as Escobar was leaving a restaurant in Medellin, he was shot repeatedly by a gunman. According to police, with each bullet the assassin was reported to have yelled "goal".

Eusebio

Mozambique born Eusebio da Silva Ferreira, know to everyone as Eusebio and to some as the 'Black Pearl', was Portugal's star turn in the 1966 World Cup. Little did he know as he travelled with his team to a decidedly chilly England that he would score nine goals during the tournament – even though Portugal would be knocked out at the semi-final stage.

Portugal won their three group games, first dispatching Hungary (3-1) then Bulgaria (3-0). Eusebio scored once against Bulgaria, but he then hit two as his side beat Brazil 3-1. After that came an extraordinary quarter-final against North Korea. At one stage Portugal were amazingly 3-0 down, but then the team got its act together and Eusebio netted four times (twice from the penalty spot)

to help secure a 5-3 victory. For this feat, the Black Pearl won a £1,000 prize – riches indeed in 1966.

In the semi-final against England, Eusebio again scored from the spot, but Bobby Charlton went one better and England won through to the Final by two goals to one. Eusebio scored a consolation penalty in the third-place playoff against the USSR, helping his side to a 2-1 win. The great Eusebio died on January 5, 2014.

Fifa

Although the English and Scottish FA were largely responsible for establishing a uniform set of rules for the game in the latter part of 19th century, neither showed much interest in extending their influence or organisational skills outside their own borders come the 20th century. This was to be a missed opportunity, for in May 1904, when representatives of Belgium, Denmark, France, Holland, Spain, Sweden and Switzerland met in Paris to discuss the formation of an international organisation, not one of the Home Country associations was in attendance, despite invitations being extended.

It was at this meeting that FIFA – Fédération Internationale de Football Association – came into being and granted to themselves responsibility for organising an international competition. The British associations were to remain aloof for a further 50 years or so, joining and then resigning over such matters as part time payments to amateurs and the re admittance of the defeated powers after the First World War.

FIFA, however, proved right from the start that they could flourish without the approval of the British: there are currently more members of FIFA than the United Nations! Although FIFA is involved in many aspects of football, including amendments to the laws and developing the game at grass-roots level, it is the organisation of the World Cup, first held in 1930 and held every four years since, world wars permitting, with which it is most closely associated.

Fontaine

It is a widely held misconception that Juste Fontaine holds the record for the most goals scored in the World Cup finals. In actual fact Fontaine's record is for scoring the most goals in a single competition, a feat achieved when he netted 13 times during the 1958 finals in Sweden.

Born in Marrakech, Morocco, on 18 August 1933, Fontaine began his professional career with US Casablanca in 1950 and spent three years with the club before moving on to OGC Nice in 1953. A tally of 44 goals in three seasons had him marked out as a proven goal scorer and in 1956 he moved on to Stade De Reims to replace the Real Madrid bound Raymond Kopa. The goals showed no sign of abating, for he hit 121 in six seasons, helping Stade De Reims win the League title in 1958 and 1960.

It is his exploits representing his country that earned Fontaine his place in football folklore, netting 30 goals in 21 matches, with his tally of 13 in six matches during the 1958 World Cup Finals, a record that has never been broken (although it has to be said that the final four goals came in

Above: *Juste Fontaine scores a goal past the Brazilian goalkeeper in the World Cup semi-final in 1958*

the third and fourth place play-off match against West Germany).

A broken leg brought his career to an end at the age of 27 and he had spells as President of the French Footballers' Union and in charge at Paris St Germain and the French national side (for two matches, both of which were lost). Although his 13 goal tally in the World Cup was eventually overtaken by Gerd Müller and Miroslav Klose (14) before Ronaldo broke the record at the 2006 Finals, Fontaine's record in one tournament may never be beaten.

France

France only took part in the first World Cup in 1930 because their very own Jules Rimet, President of FIFA, talked them into it. They beat Mexico 4-1 in Group 1, but then lost 1-0 to both Argentina and Chile. Four years later they went out to Austria in the first round, and in 1938 they lost to Italy in the second.

In 1950 they withdrew from the competition and in 1954 they failed to progress beyond the group stage. 1958 was much better: they went out 5-2 to Brazil in the semi-final, having previously beaten Paraguay 7-3 in Group 2. In the third place play-off they beat West Germany 6-3. Their performances were fairly undistinguished until 1982, when they were beaten by West Germany in the semi-final. Four years later, the Germans did for them again, once more in the semis.

There was no success in 1990 or 1994, but the 1998 World Cup finals were to be held in France. Home advantage was crucial to

the host nation, as was the fact that the other teams in Group C were amongst the weakest in the competition. They had a bit more trouble with Paraguay in the second round, winning 1-0 with a golden goal scored in extra-time, and also Italy in the quarter-final. France eventually won on penalties, when Dino Baggio missed.

In the semi-final, two goals from Thuram sealed a 2-1 victory over Croatia and the French public lapped it up. For the Final against Brazil the French team was: Brazil were badly off form for the Final and the French won it fairly easily. Two goals from the brilliant Zinedine Zidane sealed Brazil's fate, and France went on to win 3-0. The names of Barthez, Lizarazu, Desailly, Leboef, Thuram, Petit, Deschamps, Karembeu, Guivarc'h, Djorkaeff, Dugarry and Vieira also etched into folklore.

France contested the World Cup Final again in 2006 but were beaten on penalties by Italy, a game marred by an incident involving Zidane which overshadowed his retirement from a distinguished career. Their 2010 campaign was an unrivalled disaster. The scraped through qualifying, lost all their games, argued with each other in front of the world's media while the players even boycotted training.

Garrincha

Manoel dos Santos Francisco was born a cripple and retained a distorted left leg even after an operation – but he went on to win two World Cup winner's medals. Nicknamed Garrincha, meaning 'Little Songbird', because of his misshapen legs, the wayward, yet brilliant Brazilian became one of the game's best-ever right-wingers, famed for his ball skills, dribbling and 'banana' shot.

He was left out of Brazil's first two games in the 1958 finals but a players' deputation persuaded manager Vicente Feola to include him, and Garrincha played a leading role in the Final, creating his side's first two goals in the 5-2 win over Sweden. With the injured Pelé making a premature exit Garrincha became the star of the show in 1962, scoring twice against England in the quarter-final and netting another two in the semi-final win over hosts Chile. He was also sent off in that game for a retaliatory kick at Rojas. He was back for the Final, though, and Brazil went on to beat Czechoslovakia 3-1.

Garrincha returned to World Cup action in 1966, having struggled to fully recover after a motor accident, and scored a trademark free kick against Bulgaria in the opening fixture. Beset by personal problems, Garrincha died of alcohol abuse in 1983, aged only 49.

Below: *Garrincha in action against Wales, 1958*

Gascoigne

Born in Gateshead in 1967, Paul Gascoigne made his name in the 1990 World Cup and was widely regarded as the most naturally talented player to have surfaced in England for many years. He first joined Newcastle and then, in 1988, transferred to Tottenham Hotspur. He later played for Lazio, Glasgow Rangers and Middlesbrough, among others.

'Gazza' was one of England's heroes in Italia '90, even though he burst into tears when he was booked in the semi-final against Germany which his country lost on penalties: he realised that, had they won, he would have missed the Final. He nevertheless looked set for a long and brilliant career, but was a very troubled young man.

A reckless tackle in the 1991 FA Cup Final caused a career-threatening injury, but it was Gascoigne's mental state which shortened his life as a top class midfielder. Diagnosed at various times as suffering from Attention Deficit Disorder and Obsessive Compulsive Disorder, he had numerous problems off the field. England boss Bobby Robson's diagnosis was that Gazza was "daft as a brush", and that was certainly how the player appeared. He often managed to say and do the wrong thing at the wrong time, but was held in great affection by football fans everywhere. The England team could have done with many more years of Gazza – he played only 57 times for his country – and people in football everywhere continue to wish him well as continues to fight a drinking problem.

Germany

The Brazilians apart, no nation has a World Cup pedigree quite like the Germans – three times winners, four times runners-up and three times competing in the third and fourth place play-off. Absent from the first World Cup in 1930 in Uruguay, as was almost the rest of Europe, Germany made their World Cup debut in 1934 and opened their account with a 5-2 victory over the Belgians in the first round. Victory over Sweden took them to the semi-final for the first time, but Czechs proved too good and won 3-1.

Germany should have had an even stronger squad by 1938 following the Anschluss of Austria that same year but the Swiss put them out of the tournament in the first round, the only time Germany fell at the first hurdle. After being refused entrance to the 1950 tournament (the Second World War still being fresh in the memory) West Germany returned to international competition in 1954 in Switzerland. After beating Turkey 4-1 in the opening group match, Germany were hammered 8-3 by favourites Hungary (still their biggest ever defeat in the finals),

but it was something of a masterstroke by manager Sepp Herberger who fielded a weakened side, reasoning that his side could beat Turkey in a play-off and make an alternative route to the Final. So it proved, with Turkey being seen off 7-2, Yugoslavia dispatched 2-0 in the quarter-finals and Austria 6-1 in the semi-final, setting up another meeting with Hungary. The Hungarians raced into a 2-0 lead in the Final but the Germans fought back, helped by the fact that an unfit Puskas faded as the game wore on and finally scored the winning goal some six minutes before the end.

The holders came fourth in 1958, beaten in the semi-finals by hosts Sweden, meaning West Germany's next appearance in the Final was in 1966, of which more elsewhere. They claimed third place in 1970, beaten in the semi-

Above: *Morlock scores against Hungary in the World Cup Final of 1954*

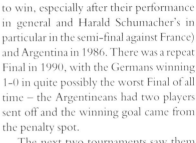

finals 4–3 by Italy in one of the best World Cup matches ever and then hosted the 1974 tournament, winning six matches on their way to lifting the trophy (their only defeat came in a group match against the East Germans!) and beating favourites Holland into the bargain.

They won only one match in Argentina in 1978, going out in the second group stage, and then made three consecutive appearances in the Final, losing to Italy in 1982 (they didn't deserve

to win, especially after their performance in general and Harald Schumacher's in particular in the semi-final against France) and Argentina in 1986. There was a repeat Final in 1990, with the Germans winning 1-0 in quite possibly the worst Final of all time – the Argentineans had two players sent off and the winning goal came from the penalty spot.

The next two tournaments saw them eliminated at the quarter-final stage, their worst run ever, and they weren't much better in 2002, after emerging from their group unbeaten, they were beaten by the Brazilians in the Final. Hosting the 2006 World Cup expectations were extremely high after beating Argentina 4-2 on penalties they progressed to the semi-finals to face Italy. The semi-final between Germany and Italy produced a riveting extra-time period, scoreless until the 118th minute, when Italy scored twice to put an end to Germany's undefeated record in Dortmund. In 2010, Germany again finished an unwanted third after a 3-2 win over Uruguay.

Gerrard

Pelé once said of Steven Gerrard: "To me he is one of the super best midfielders in the world. He is an excellent player." How England would love Gerrard to shine in the great Brazilian's backyard in 2014.

One of the greatest midfielders in the English game, Gerrard has made himself one of Liverpool's legends. He scored his first international goal in 2001, during England's tumultuous 5-1 win over Germany in Munich. Simply, he is a lynchpin for both club and country.

With Liverpool failing to lift trophies, there was talk of Gerrard leaving Anfield. But with Rafael Benitez installed as Liverpool manager, he became the youngest captain ever to hold aloft the European Cup as Liverpool defeated AC Milan in 2005's unforgettable Champions League final in Istanbul.

After he was announced as the PFA's player of the year 12 months later, his leadership – as well as tireless running – helped Liverpool reach another Champions League final in 2007, again against Milan.

Gerrard's performances for England have been more erratic, despite his pivotal role at the 2004 European Championships and the 2006 World Cup.

However, he missed a penalty in the shoot-out against Portugal in the quarter-final defeat at the 2006 tournament and failed to bond with Frank Lampard in central midfield.

Yet, he remains England's talisman figure. Whether Hodgson and Gerrard, in his last World Cup, can turn around England's fortunes on the world stage is another matter altogether.

Above: *Steven Gerrard of England celebrates scoring his team's second goal during the FIFA 2010 World Cup*

Hagi

Having been a fully-fledged Romanian international from the age of 18, Gheorghe Hagi paraded his midfield brilliance and sublime left foot in three World Cup finals, the first of which was the 1990 tournament in Italy. Nicknamed the 'Maradona of the Carpathians', Hagi was a worthy peer of the stocky Argentine both for his talents and fiery temperament.

However, even though that 1990 showing helped him secure a £2m move to Real Madrid, it was at the 1994 finals in America that really made his mark. A 40-yard lob in Romania's 3-1 victory against Columbia in his side's opening fixture was exquisitely delivered. And the midfield general proved he was at the peak of his career by inspiring Romania to a 3-2 success over Argentina in the second round. Hagi orchestrated a flowing move upfield and was on hand to lay on the final pass for Ilie Dunitrescu to give Romania an early lead. Hagi then scored twice to ensure his side progressed. Another thrilling encounter followed in the quarter-finals – a 2-2 draw against Sweden – only this time Romania bowed out of the competition after a penalty shoot-out. Hagi's impact on Romanian football was enormous: he won his country's Player of the Year award a record six times and was even named Player of the Century.

Hodgson

Roy Hodgson was appointed England's 13th manager on 1 May 2012. Born on August 9, 1947, the hugely experienced Hodgson has coached in many parts of the world, while England is the fourth national team he has managed.

His 36-year career as a manager began with Swedish club Halmstad in 1976. He had three years in charge of Switzerland, guiding them to the last 16 of the 1994 World Cup in America and taking them to Euro 96, though he had left his role before the Finals. Switzerland's progression under Hodgson was clear in the statistics: the Swiss hadn't qualified for a major tournament since the 1960s.

An old-school coach with interests outside of football – he reads highbrow literature and speaks several languages - Hodgson brings a quiet dignity and charm to the position. Unlike previous England managers, he has not been partial to the typical roasting handed out by the British media, too.

At club level Hodgson managed a host of top clubs: Inter Milan and Udinese, Blackburn Rovers, Malmo, FC Copenhagen and Grasshopper. In 2007 he took over the helm at Fulham, before joining Liverpool in an ill-fated tenure.

In late 2013, Hodgson and former England defender Rio Ferdinand were appointed to the FA's commission to improve the state of the national game. He could do it all himself at the 2014 World Cup Finals if Hodgson were to lead England all the way to glory and banish the blues which have hung over the national side since 1966.

Holland

As Brazil in 1938 and 1950 and Hungary in 1954, among others found out to their cost, the best side does not always win the World Cup. Much the same fate befell the Dutch, widely regarded as the best team in the world in 1974 and nearly as highly regarded in 1978, yet on both occasions they left the World Cup finals with nothing more than runners-up medals to show for their efforts.

Holland made their first World Cup appearances in 1934 and 1938, going out in the first round on both occasions. They

did not bother to participate in 1950 and 1954 and failed to qualify for any of the next four tournaments. By 1974 however, the side that featured the likes of Johan Cruyff, Johan Neeskens, Ruud Krol and Johnny Rep, guided by coach Rinus Michels and playing 'total football' (where every player was expected to attack and defend in equal measure) had them listed among the favourites.

The tag sat happily on the Dutch as they powered their way to the Final, beating Sweden, Bulgaria and Uruguay in their first group matches and then Brazil, Argentina and East Germany in the second group. That earned them a Final appearance against the West Germans, and Lady Luck continued to smile on the Dutch as the game kicked off – within a minute Johan Cruyff was hauled down in the penalty area and a spot kick awarded.

Neeskens duly dispatched it home and it appeared as though the Dutch would be lifting the new trophy aloft come the final whistle. But a Breitner penalty and Gerd Müller goal won it for Germany.

The Dutch weren't quite so impressive four years later (there was no Cruyff this time around, who refused to go because of the political situation in Argentina at the time), winning only one of their initial group matches, against Iran, but by a big enough score to mean that defeat against the Scots 3-2 did not hinder their progress into the second group stage. Holland won the all-European group against Austria, Italy and West Germany (revenge was sweet), to make the Final against the hosts. This time it was the Dutch who had to come from behind, equalising through substitute Dick Nanninga eight minutes from time. In injury time Resenbrink could have won it for the Dutch, but hit the post, and the reprieved Argentineans saw off the Dutch with two extra-time goals.

That was as good as it got for the Dutch as a sequence of failing to qualify and poor results throughout the nineties and into the early noughties saw them struggle to garner any improvement. There were hopes in advance of the 2006 World Cup

in Germany but were beaten in the last 16 by Portugal in a stormy encounter. Both teams finished the game with nine men in a game which equalled the World Cup record for bookings – 16 – and broke the record for red cards.

The Dutch experienced the same storm in 2010, but this time it came in the final – their first since 1978. Referee Howard Webb handed out 14 cards, including a red for John Heitinga, before Spain won it in injury time through Andres Iniesta.

Above: *The victorious hosts Uruguay, in the 1930 World Cup Final*

Hosts

Perhaps only twice has sentiment been allowed to dictate which nation should host the FIFA World Cup – the very first tournament in 1930, and again in 1966. Seven nations offered to host the first tournament when FIFA met in 1928 to discuss the matter; six from Europe and one from South America. The South American nation of Uruguay had won the Olympic football tournament (one that was organised by FIFA after the First World War) twice in succession in 1924 and 1928, and would be celebrating their 100th anniversary of independence in1930. This, coupled with their offer to fund the entire costs of the tournament, including travel expenses for all contestants, was sufficient to earn them the honour in 1930.

Thereafter it was Europe that held sway, not least because it accounted for the more powerful members of FIFA, including its executive committee, and saw Italy and France host the tournament in 1934 and 1938. With Europe ravaged by war in 1942 and 1946, when the tournament would have been held, and still in the throes of recovery in 1950, the finals returned to South America, this time in Brazil, in 1950.

The idea of alternating the finals between Europe and South America did not begin in earnest until 1962 when the finals went to Chile. The following tournament, in England in 1966, was probably awarded to help the English FA, the oldest of all associations in the world celebrate their centenary, which had occurred in 1963.

The growing abilities of first African, then Asian countries saw them lobby not only for increased participation in the Finals but also the opportunity of hosting the event. Germany hosted the tournament in 2006 and South Africa were awarded the 2010 Finals. However, FIFA has also gone into new territories following the decision to award the 2018 and 2022 World Cups to Russia and Qatar respectively.

Above: *Hungary play Italy in the 1938 World Cup Final in France*

Below: *Hungarian goalkeeper Gelei, gets ready to catch the ball in the 1966 World Cup finals*

Hungary

Like Holland, the Hungarians might have won the World Cup twice, should have won it once and yet have little to show for their efforts over the last 80 years or so. They made their first appearance in the finals in 1934, losing to the Austrians in the quarter-final. Four years later they had a fairly simple run-in to the Final in France. It was perhaps the Hungarians' misfortune to meet an Italian side that was even better than the one that had lifted the trophy in 1934 and they lost 4-2.

After failing to enter in 1950, Hungary returned to the world stage four years later. They had been unbeaten since 1950; a run that included defeats of England (6-3 at Wembley and then 7-1 in Budapest) and they arrived at the 1954 tournament in Switzerland as undoubted favourites. Four straight victories, with 25 goals scored and only seven conceded set up a Final against the West Germans. This, however, was a different West German side to the one that had gone down 8-3 in the group, for key players had been rested. Also Puskas was not fully fit and shouldn't have played; he faded as the game wore on. Still it started brightly for the Hungarians, who took a 2-0 lead inside eight minutes only to be pegged back and overtaken. Puskas had a goal disallowed two minutes from time before the whistle indicated Hungary's first defeat in 30 matches in their most important match of all.

The Revolution of 1956 did almost as much as advancing years to break up that wonderful side and Hungary has struggled to make an impact on the game ever since. Reaching the quarterfinals in both 1962 and 1966 remains the peak of Hungarian achievement since 1954, and in their three appearances in 1978, 1982 and 1986 they have failed to advance beyond the group stages. That they failed to do so in 1982 remains something of a mystery, for in their first match they beat El Salvador 10-1 to register the biggest score in a World Cup finals match.

Hurst

Geoffrey Charles Hurst, whose goals won the 1966 World Cup Final for England, was born in Ashton-under-Lyne in 1941. He spent most of his club career with West Ham United, for whom he scored 180 goals in 411 League appearances.

Hurst's first international appearance was against West Germany, only five months before the 1966 World Cup finals. He was at first regarded as a reserve striker for the competition, and many felt sorry for Jimmy Greaves when the latter was not included in the line-up for the Final against West Germany, but it turned out that Alf Ramsey had got it right. Having netted the equaliser early in the game, Hurst scored England's much-disputed third goal in extra time, courtesy of linesman Bakhramov, who was sure the ball had crossed the line as it bounced down from the crossbar. On such decisions are World Cups won and lost.

Hurst's third goal came from a breakaway near the end, as the Germans pressed for another equaliser. It went down in broadcasting history for inspiring Kenneth Wolstenholme's immortal comment: "They think it's all over – it is now." As well as being the first player to score a hat-trick in a World Cup Final, Geoff Hurst – who had played cricket for Essex – became the only county cricketer to win a World Cup winners' medal.

Above: *Hurst jumps in jubilation after scoring England's winning goal against Argentina in the World Cup quarter-final in 1966*

Ireland

The Republic of Ireland made little impact on the international scene until 1988, even though the country had produced formidable players like Liam Brady, Ronnie Whelan and David O'Leary.

Honorary Irishman Jack Charlton took over as manager in 1986. He realised that he did not have enough home-grown players to enable his side to do well in major competitions, so he set about recruiting players like John Aldridge and Ray Houghton, who were unlikely to play for their own country, but who had some Irish ancestry. The plan paid off, and Charlton's first major success came in a European Championship group game when Houghton headed his side to a 1-0 victory over England.

In 1990, the Republic reached the World Cup quarter-finals, drawing 1-1 with England along the way. It was a fine achievement, but the Irish lost to Italy by a single Schillaci goal. Four years later they again reached the final stages, where this time they beat Italy with a Houghton goal in a group game, but lost to Mexico and drew with Norway.

In 2002 manager Mick McCarthy took the Republic into the last 16, where Robbie Keane scored from the spot against Spain, but the team lost out 3-2 on penalties. Giovanni Trapattoni then presided over the Republic's qualification play-off defeat before the 2010 World Cup to France when Thierry Henry controversially handballed in creating a goal for his side.

Italy

Italy are one of the most successful nations when it comes to the World Cup, having lifted the trophy on three occasions and been beaten Finalists twice. They made their first impact on the tournament in 1934, which following lobbying by dictator Benito Mussolini, was held in Italy.

Had the Czechoslovakians shut up shop, as Italy would do with regularity for many years after, they would have held on to win, but in pressing forward for a second goal allowed gaps to appear in their defence. One of these was seized upon by Raimondo Orsi (actually an Argentinean) eight minutes from time, taking the game into extra time, and Angelo Schiavo scored the winner, much to the delight of the majority of the 55,000 crowd, which included dictator Benito Mussolini.

Perhaps Italy's best performance in 1938 came in the semi-final against Brazil, a match the Brazilians were widely expected to win but overconfidence did for them; they left out top goalscorer Leonidas da Silva from the semi in order that he would be fresh for the Final. A 2-1 victory for Italy meant Leonidas was

rested for nothing and Italy had a Final against Hungary to look forward to. In one of the more entertaining games of the tournament, Italy won 4-2 in a match where they were seldom troubled.

Italy were to hold on to the trophy for 12 years, the outbreak of the Second World War meaning there was no competition until 1950. In 1962 they qualified for the finals in Chile, but this was the Italians at their most cynical when they were losing 2-0 to the hosts in the infamous Battle of Santiago. Four years later came shame of a different kind as they slipped out of the competition following defeat by the North Koreans. Although the flight taking the players home was supposed to be landing at a secret destination, disgruntled fans found out and hurled rotten vegetables at the players as they stepped off the plane.

They made amends of sorts four years

Above: Alfredo Foni of Italy (left) tries to reach a cross in the World Cup Final against Hungary in 1938

goals from Paolo Rossi secured them a place in the Final against West Germany, and Rossi was to score again in a 3-1 victory. Their defence of the trophy lasted until the second round in 1986, beaten by France, but there were high hopes of a victory in 1990, when the tournament finals returned to Italy after an absence of 56 years. The dream lasted until the semi-final, beaten 4-3 on penalties by Argentina. Penalties did for the Italians four years later, against Brazil in the Final in the USA. It was a similar story in France in 1998 with France winning on penalties and so to the 2002 tournament where defeat came in the second round at the hands of South Korea. In 2006, Italy beat France 5-3 in a penalty shoot-out to win the World Cup and become the most successful European team in World Cup history. Fabio Grosso scored the winning penalty after France's David Trezeguet missed. The result capped an incredible period for Italian football, with the domestic game embroiled in a corruption scandal similar to 1982 when they last won the World Cup.

later, reaching the Final against Brazil, but Italy winning would have been a travesty – they qualified top of their group despite scoring only one goal in three matches. The Brazilians produced a masterful display in the final, winning 4-1.

The two countries met again in 1978, although this was for third and fourth place in a tournament destined to be won by Argentina, and once again the Brazilians proved too good, winning 2-1. By 1982 there was a new Italy in evidence, one that did not rely so much on defensive strength, however they did not win a single group match and only advanced by virtue of having scored one more goal than Cameroon.

It was in the second group phase that they came into their own, beating holders Argentina and favourites Brazil (at last) to make the semi-finals against Poland. Two

Disaster struck four years later though as they crashed out of South Africa 2010, finishing bottom, behind New Zealand, in their group with two points.

Jairzinho

J air Ventura Filho – Jairzinho – became a worthy successor to his boyhood hero and right-wing wizard Garrincha. The pair played together briefly for Brazil in the 1966 World Cup, with Jairzinho playing well within himself on the left flank. After recovering from a twice-broken right leg he was restored to his favoured right-wing berth for the 1970 tournament in Mexico and took the spotlight as Brazil's awesome side imperiously swept aside all challengers to lift the trophy for the third time.

To shine in such company as Carlos Alberto, Rivelino, Tostao, Gerson and the inimitable Pelé took some doing but Jairzinho managed that with his electric turn of pace and powerful shooting – and the record-breaking feat of scoring in every match. He scored seven in all, starting with a brace in Brazil's opening victory over Czechoslovakia. Later in the competition his was the deciding strike in a classic confrontation with England, taking a measured lay-off from Pelé before firing past the seemingly unbeatable Gordon Banks.

Jairzinho sealed his goalscoring record in the Final with a 70th minute strike against Italy as Brazil cantered to a 4-1 success. He also appeared in the 1974 finals, scoring against both Zaire and Argentina, but he and his fellow Brazilians had to settle for fourth place.

Above: *Jairzinho rounds Luis Rubinos of Peru to score the fourth goal for Brazil, during the World Cup quarter-final, 1970*

Japan

Japan did not qualify for a World Cup finals tournament until 1998, when a 3-2 win in sudden-death time enabled them to beat Iran in the third and fourth place play-off. It was rather good timing, for Japan was scheduled to co-host the 2002 tournament with South Korea, where both nations would qualify automatically.

On the face of it their record of three defeats in their three group matches and bottom of the table looked no more than they could have expected, but Japan actually gave a rather good account of themselves. They certainly enjoyed their debut on the world stage, for all three defeats were by a single-goal deficit, against Argentina, Croatia and Jamaica. Four years later, spared the trouble of qualifying,

Japan went a stage further. Not only that, but they managed to win their group, knocking out the much-fancied Russians into the bargain. Their tournament began with a draw, 2-2, against Belgium (as fancied as the Russians). Five days later came the shock of a single goal victory over Russia thanks to the European-based Junichi Inamoto, and five days after that a 2-0 win over Tunisia, while the Belgians were beating Russia 3-2, was enough to lift Japan to the top of Group H.

After going out in the second-round clash with Turkey, Japan looked forward to qualification for Germany 2006 but were disappointed to go out of the tournament without a single win. They made amends in 2010 by reaching the last 16 before being knocked-out on penalties against Paraguay.

Kempes

Argentine striker Mario Kempes played 18 times in three World Cup finals. Although he failed to find the net in the 1974 and 1982 tournaments he was the outstanding performer and top goalscorer in the 1978 event staged in his home country. He produced a match-winning performance in the Final against Holland, scoring twice as Argentina won 3-1.

A first-half strike by Kempes gave the host nation the lead only for a late equaliser to take the game into extra time. With the match looking for a hero, up stepped Kempes to score a superb solo goal, taking on three Dutch defenders before slotting the ball home. The victory was rubber-stamped when another positive run culminated in Kempes setting up Daniel Bertoni for the third goal. Earlier in the competition he netted

twice against Poland in the second round and grabbed another brace in the 6-0 trouncing of Peru.

Having been transferred to Valencia in 1976, Kempes paved the way for his World Cup-winning exploits by becoming the Spanish League's top goalscorer for two successive years. His total of 24 goals in his debut season was the league's highest in ten years, but he topped this with 28 the following season, the best total since Alfredo Di Stefano's 31 in 1956-57.

Above: *Kempes celebrates scoring against Holland during the World Cup Final, 1978*

Right: *Klinsmann out climbs an Argentinean defender during the World Cup Final, 1990*

Klinsmann

Now installed as USA coach, Jürgen Klinsmann continues his love affair with the World Cup after the winners' medal he picked up in 1990.

He made his international debut for Germany in a 1-1 draw with Brazil in 1987 and went on to become one of the world's best strikers, plying his trade in Germany, France, England and Italy.

Twice Footballer of the Year in Germany (1988, 1994) and once in England (1995), Klinsmann's raids on opposition defences were nothing if not eye-catching. His greatest performance was probably in 1990 against Holland in the second round. The blond hitman was seemingly everywhere and gave Germany the lead after 50 minutes with a clever header and later struck a post as Italy were eventually defeated 2-1. The Final, against Argentina, was nowhere near as good a contest, a niggly, defensive affair decided by a penalty. Klinsmann, though, felt the full force of a shocking second-half tackle by Pedro Monzon, who was sent off.

Germany had a disappointing campaign four years later at USA '94,

exiting at the quarter-final stage, but Klinsmann was a major success. He then made a surprise move to Tottenham Hotspur where he not only overcame a reputation for theatrics but won over the sceptical English fans with his humour, grace and a sackful of goals. Klinsmann captained Germany to triumph at Euro 96 in England and scored three goals as the Germans reached the 1998 quarter-finals before retiring.

He went on to coach Germany from 2004-06, leading the team to third in their home World Cup and joined the US in 2011.

Korea (North and South)

It says much for the development of the game in Asia over the last 50 or so years that in 2002 the continent could boast 44 members of FIFA, of whom 42 entered into the World Cup. Compare this with 1954 – just three teams; Japan, South Korea and China, entered, and the Chinese withdrew before kicking a ball. South Korea won 7-3 on aggregate to claim the lone Asian place in the finals in Switzerland and were pitched into a group with Hungary, West Germany and Turkey. Because of the seeding system in operation, South Korea were only expected to play two matches, against Hungary and Turkey, and lost both heavily, 9-0 against the Hungarians and 7-0 against Turkey.

The Koreans were then absent from the competition finals until 1966, but this time it was their political foes from North Korea who qualified. The Asian, African and Australia qualifying competition was to have involved 20 nations, but 16 African states withdrew and South Africa were suspended because

Above: *Shin Yong Kyoo and goalkeeper Chan Myung of North Korea block a shot by Eusebio of Portugal in the World Cup quarter-final, 1966*

of violating anti-discrimination rules left only three countries to compete for the last spot in the tournament. South Korea withdrew at the last minute (they claimed they wished to concentrate on the 1968 Olympic competition), leaving North Korea and Australia to battle it out.

Two victories in Cambodia, 6-1 and 3-1, saw the North Koreans qualify. Their record of one win, one draw and one defeat would have had them heading home in double-quick time in any other group, but in Group 4, the victory over Italy and draw against Chile was enough to earn them a place in the quarter-finals. The 3-0 defeat against Russia in their opening match counted for little in the final group placings, but it did reveal

flaws in their defence, flaws that were eventually to cause their undoing in the quarterfinal against Portugal.

After a quarter of an hour the Koreans were three goals ahead and seemingly on their way to the semis, but then Portugal in general and Eusebio in particular woke up and began to pull the match back, scoring twice before half time and three times after (Eusebio helping himself to four goals, two from the penalty spot) to bring North Korea's journey to an end. They have yet to retrace their steps.

South Korea meanwhile re-appeared in Italy in 1990, only to lose all three matches and finish bottom of the group. Four years later they had improved enough to gain creditable draws against Spain and Bolivia, but defeat against Germany still saw them eliminated. In France in 1998 there was only one draw, against Belgium, before they went home again to prepare for the 2002 tournament, where they were joint hosts with Japan.

On home territory South Korea were the real surprise package, progressing further than anyone could have hoped or dreamed of. They topped their group, seeing off the Portuguese and Poles into the bargain, and then beat Italy 2-1 in sudden death and Spain on penalties to make the semi-finals. There they were finally undone by the Germans, but as a measure of how far they had come since 1954, they only lost 1-0.

Qualifying for four successive tournaments (even if they were automatic qualifiers in 2002) shows that South Korea are one of the emerging nations in the game, and they confirmed this by making it eight in a row for Brazil 2014.

Lampard

Frank Lampard's record in the World Cup – like most contemporary English players – is not particularly special but it will always be remembered for something that didn't happen in a match in the 2010 Finals. Against arch rivals Germany, his long range shot hit the crossbar and clearly bounced over the line but was not awarded. With the world watching on TV, it seemed that the only people who didn't see the ball cross the line were the referee and linesman. Whilst England also lost the match, the cancelled goal helped prompt the introduction of goal-line technology so that incidents such as this didn't happen again in major tournaments.

Lampard also had mixed emotions in England's 2006 World Cup campaign. In the first game of the tournament against Paraguay, he was named Man of the Match as England won 1–0. Though he played every minute of England's matches, he went scoreless as the team were eliminated in the quarterfinals by Portugal on penalties, and he was one of the three players who missed their spot

Above: *Frank Lampard*

kicks, alongside Steven Gerrard and Jamie Carragher.

His unlucky streak continued in the 2010 tournament when he made 37 shots on goal without scoring, more than any other player since 1966. With more than 100 England caps to his credit, he is an England legend and it would be fitting if he could find the net at least once in the Brazil tournament – that is if he is picked for the squad and the ball also crosses the line!

Laurent

Frenchman Lucien Laurent wrote himself into World Cup history in 1930 by scoring the competition's first ever goal, a volley in the 19th minute against Mexico on 13 July in Montevideo. France won 4-1, but lost group matches to Argentina and Chile. Inside-forward Laurent had missed the third group game in 1930 due to a foul in the previous game from Argentinean centre-half Luisito Monti. There were no substitutes, and the French might well have reversed the slim 1-0 deficit had he been fit.

Lucien, whose brother Jean also played for France, failed to grace the 1934 World Cup, again through injury. His club career saw him moving from Sochaux to Rennes, then RC Strasbourg until 1939. Captured by the Germans, he spent three years as a prisoner of war but was liberated to play wartime football for Besançon. After retirement in 1946, Laurent became a youth football coach.

Born on 10 December 10, 1907 in St Maur, Val de Marne near Paris, he played 10 times in total for France, scoring twice, and was the only surviving member of the 1930 national side who lived to see France claim the World Cup on home soil. As an amateur, he only received minimal expenses from his country's football federation, a far cry from the pampered superstars of today. He died on 11 April 2005 in Besançon.

Right: *Sandor Kocsis of Hungary, leading scorer in the 1954 World Cup*

Far Right: *The Golden Boot trophy awarded to the World Cup's highest scorer*

Below: *Argentinean forward Guillermo Stabile was top scorer in the first World Cup 1930*

Leading Goalscorers

A longside actually winning the trophy, the competition to finish the tournament's top goalscorer is one of the most keenly contested. It says much for the quality of the competition over its seven decades that no player has finished top goalscorer twice, and even some of the biggest names of football failed to achieve the feat even once, including Pelé, England's record goalscorer Bobby Charlton and the prolific Jimmy Greaves.

It was Guillermo Stabile of Argentina who set the benchmark for all future goalscorers, netting eight times in the first tournament in Uruguay in 1930. He also became one of the first players to score a hat trick in the World Cup, netting three times in Argentina's 6-3 win over Mexico, and moved to Europe to ply his trade after the tournament, in which Argentina were runners-up. The bar

was raised in 1950 when the Brazilian Ademir netted nine goals as Brazil also finished runners-up, a tally that included four goals in the 7-1 win over Sweden in the Final pool match. Sandor Kocsis of Hungary scored 11 in 1954, although once again could only collect a runners-up medal for his efforts. He had scored two goals in the bitter quarter Final clash with Brazil to draw level with Ademir, and then two extra-time goals in the victory over Uruguay to move into pole position. Unfortunately he was unable to add to his tally in the Final as West Germany came from behind to win 3-2.

It was in Sweden in 1958 that Juste Fontaine scored his 13 goals to establish the record goalscoring achievement in a single tournament, netting four goals in the third and fourth place play-off. Since then only one player has reached double figures in a single World Cup finals tournament, Gerd Müller in 1970 in Mexico netting 10 goals as West Germany reached the semi-final. Four years later Müller scored a further four goals taking his tally to 14 goals. Meanwhile, Miroslav Klose's four goals at the 2006 tournament meant he finished his career with 14. But these were overtaken by Brazilian Ronaldo – with 15 goals – during the 2006 World Cup to take top place.

Pele's tally of 13 was achieved across four World Cup tournaments (1958, 1962, 1966, and 1970) with Ronaldo also appearing in four, (1994, 1998, 2002 and 2006). The only Englishman to appear on the list is Gary Lineker, with 10 goals, although he did finish the 1986 tournament as top scorer with six.

Lineker

Gary Winston Lineker was born in Leicester in 1960. He played for his beloved Leicester City, scoring more than 100 goals in just under 200 League games, before moving to Everton, Barcelona and Tottenham Hotspur. His England tally was a more than respectable 48 in 80 matches.

What was probably his finest hour came in the heat and humidity of the 1986 World Cup in Mexico. He missed a few scoring chances in England's opening Group F game, in which his side went down 1-0 to Portugal and, together with everyone else, he failed to score in a 0-0 draw with Morocco. But then came a must win game for England in which Lineker became the first English player to score a World Cup hat-trick since Geoff Hurst accomplished it in 1966. England won 3-0 and squeezed into the next round,

where Lineker scored two more as his side ran out 3-2 victors over Paraguay.

England's quarter-final tie was the infamous game against Argentina. Lineker scored his team's only goal, but Argentina won 2-1. Four years later, when England reached the semi-finals, Lineker scored in the 1-1 draw with Germany, before the Germans went on to win the match 4-3 on penalties.

The erudite Lineker's playing days ended in Japan, but he has since become an accomplished television presenter.

Maradona

Right:
*Maradona's rather
dubious 'Hand
of God' goal for
Argentina, 1986*

Born in 1960 to a poor family and brought up one of eight children, Diego Armando Maradona overcame his upbringing to become the most gifted footballer of his generation. He was playing professional football by the time he was 16 and went on to star in four World Cup campaigns, leading his country Argentina from the front – and as coach from the bench, in 2010, when they reached the last eight.

His first World Cup, in Spain in 1982, was notable for obtaining him a £1.7 million transfer to Barcelona, impressed with what they saw. By the 1986 tournament in Mexico he was a Naples player, and was at his international peak: he steered his country to victory, though the competition will be remembered also for his 'Hand of God' goal against England. Four years later in Italy he managed to take his country to the Final once more, though this time West Germany, 3-2 losers in '86, had their revenge. In 1994 he was sent home from the United States in disgrace having failed a drugs test and the rags to riches dream was over.

Like many other great players, Best and Gascoigne among them, Maradona failed to cope with life outside football. He seems to have become addicted to almost everything one can become addicted to and, on several occasions in recent years, his life has hung in the balance. In 2000, FIFA declared him the joint best ever player alongside Pelé: the comparison is a fascinating one.

Meazza

Nicknamed Peppino, Guiseppe Meazza was a stalwart of the Italian side that clinched two consecutive World Cups in the 1930s. Born in Milan in 1910, Meazza initially made his name as a centre-forward with Inter but it was when national manager Vittorio Pozzo moved him to inside-forward that he found his best position. He scored twice on his 1930 debut against Switzerland and was a vital component of the Italian team that emulated Uruguay's victory in the first tournament when, as hosts, they won the 1934 World Cup, the first to be held in Europe. He was captain when they became the first nation to retain the trophy four years later but the Second World War put paid to any chance of a hat-trick.

Injury wrecked Meazza's 1938-39 season that preceded a move to rivals AC Milan. He guested for Juventus and Varese during the hostilities before finishing his fulltime playing career with Atalanta in 1945, although he donned his boots on

a few occasions while managing Inter. Meazza's record of 33 goals in 53 games stood for almost 30 years until beaten by Luigi Riva in 1973, while his total of 269 goals in 440 Serie A appearances also remains impressive.

Above: Captain Giuseppe Meazza (left) shakes hands with Hungarian captain Gyorgy Sarosi, at the start of the World Cup Final in 1938

Menotti

Best remembered as the chain-smoking, tough talking manager of 1978 World champions Argentina, Cesar Luis Menotti was born in Rosario on 5 November 1938. As a player, 'El Flaco' (in recognition of his thin appearance) began his career with local club Rosario and proved an accomplished striker, netting 47 goals in 86 appearances before a move to the higher profile Racing Club in 1964. He had later spells playing in the USA and Brazil, but it is perhaps as a manager that he made his biggest mark.

Not afraid of making unpopular decisions (such as leaving the burgeoning Diego Maradona out of the 1978 squad), Menotti was single minded about what he wanted from his team. No-one was allowed to influence him in any way. This included journalists – 'Not only do they not know anything about football, but if you were to shut them up in a room by themselves, they couldn't even write a letter to mother.' Menotti was vindicated when his side went on to lift the trophy at the 1978 tournament, with a joyous attacking philosophy.

After the competition, Menotti moved into club management, taking over the reins at Boca Juniors (on two occasions), River Plate, Barcelona and Sampdoria and more recently Independiente, his third spell in charge of the famous Argentinean club, until he quit in 2010.

Mexico

Left: *Hugo Sanchez performs a hand stand in the game against Norway, 1994*

Based on their overall performance in World Cup Finals, Mexico are the 13th most successful nation, but they have yet to make even a semi-final, indicative of a nation that flatters to deceive. Indeed, although they competed or qualified in the tournaments of 1930, 1950, 1954, 1958 and 1962, it was not until their last group match of 1962 that they actually won. By then the 3-1 win over Czechoslovakia meant nothing; Mexico headed home as the Czechs headed towards the Final.

In 1970 Mexico finally managed to advance beyond the group stage, but as host nation they were expected to. Despite beating El Salvador and Belgium and drawing with the Soviet Union in the group, Italy gave them a lesson and a 4-1 beating in the quarterfinal. They failed to qualify in 1974, lost all three matches in 1978 and were then absent until 1986. Again, it was as hosts (Colombia, the original choice, having withdrawn), and again Mexico made the quarter-final (albeit with one extra qualifying round) before being knocked out on penalties by West Germany.

Mexico failed to qualify in 1990 but there has since been a marked improvement in their performances. While they have yet to advance beyond the second round, they have given all of their opponents a close run for their money – Bulgaria in 1994 won on penalties, Germany in 1998 by a single goal and the USA (themselves much improved over recent years) won by 2-0 when the Mexicans were chasing the game in 2002.

Milla

Six goals from Roger Milla in the 1982 World Cup qualifiers helped to take Cameroon to the finals for the first time. But it was not until 1990 that the world sat up to take real notice of both the country and the player. Milla, aged 38, became the star of the side in Italy, scoring four times as a 'super-sub' to spearhead the Cameroon charge to the quarter-finals. One of the over-riding memories of the tournament was Milla performing his celebratory dance around the corner flag every time he scored.

The Indomitable Lions scored a shock win over Argentina then ensured qualification to the next stage with a 2-1 win over Romania; Milla scored both goals, becoming the oldest goalscorer in the World Cup finals. The striker repeated the feat in the 2-1 win over Colombia and was involved in both Cameroon goals as they were squeezed out of the competition by England, 3-2.

Incredibly Milla, aged 42, was back with Cameroon at USA '94 and, when he netted against Russia he extended his own record as the World Cup's oldest scorer. There was no happy ending though – Russia won 6-1.

Moore

England's only World Cup-winning captain, Robert Frederick Chelsea Moore, was born in Barking in 1941. A fine central defender, he spent most of his League career at West Ham, ending his playing days in this country with Fulham, where he captained the Cottagers to an FA Cup Final appearance in 1975. It seems that his dad was a Chelsea supporter, but Chelsea were not to feature in Bobby Moore's career.

Moore won a record 108 England caps during his illustrious career, 90 of them as captain. One of three West Ham players in the victorious World Cup winning side, it was he who held the trophy aloft at Wembley Stadium in 1966, having laid

Below: *Moore, Hurst and Peters of England (and West Ham) can't believe that they've won the World Cup in 1966*

on two of Geoff Hurst's goals. He was later voted Player of the Tournament.

Widely respected throughout the world of football, Moore was ludicrously accused of stealing a bracelet in Bogota, prior to the 1970 World Cup finals in Mexico. Somebody, it seemed, did not want him to play. But play he did,

captaining his side through to the unfortunate 3-2 defeat by West Germany in the quarter-finals.

Moore won many of the game's honours, but his talents could have been better used after he retired from playing. Sadly, he died of cancer in 1993, at the all too early age of 52.

Left: *Müller celebrates scoring in the World Cup Final, 1974*

Müller

Stockily-built and with tree-trunk legs, Gerd Müller simply came alive in the opposition penalty area – with a staggering 68 goals in 62 international appearances for West Germany he was a goal-poaching sensation.

In 15 seasons with Bayern Munich the man they called 'Der Bomber' rattled in 365 goals in 427 games – and yet his first coach at Bayern, Zlato Cajovski was none too impressed with his appearance, saying: 'I'm not putting that little elephant in among my string of thoroughbreds.' He did, though, and Bayern and Müller, who topped the Bundesliga scoring charts in seven seasons, never looked back. Müller made his international bow against Turkey in 1966 and enjoyed a wonderful 1970 World Cup in Mexico. He netted ten goals in six games, including successive hat-tricks against Bulgaria and Peru, and it was his extra-time strike that sealed a 3-2 comeback win over England in the quarterfinals. Müller did his bit in the semi-final clash with Italy with two extra-time goals, but the Germans were pipped 4-3.

Although not as prolific when the World Cup came to Germany in 1974, Müller came up with a late strike to help see off Poland in the semi-final then typically made the most of a half chance to score the winner in the Final as the Germans beat Holland 2-1.

Neeskens

While Johan Cruyff got most of the adulation from the media and fans who admired the almost all-conquering Dutch side of the 1970s, it was Johan Neeskens who was the midfield powerhouse that made it all possible. Born in Heemstede on 15 September 1951 he began his career with local club RCH before linking with Cruyff at Ajax in 1969.

With Neeskens and Cruyff effectively directing operations, Ajax became one of the most successful club sides in Europe, and this combination went on to repeat their relationship at international level. First capped in 1970, Neeskens was an integral part of the side that reached the World Cup Final in 1974, scoring five goals along the way, including Holland's penalty in the Final. After the Final he left Ajax for Barcelona (Cruyff had made a similar move a year previously!) and helped them win the European Cup Winners Cup in 1978-79. By then Neeskens had competed in his second World Cup Finals tournament, in Argentina.

While Cruyff was absent on conscientious grounds when the 1978 World Cup came around, Neeskens was still a regular fixture in the side, albeit occupying a more defensive midfield role, as evidenced by the fact he failed to score in this competition. Holland however made the Final a second time, only to lose a second to the hosts. In 1979 Johan moved to America to play for New York Cosmos, finishing his playing career in 1986 with three European Cup winners medals, a World Club Championship and two runners-up medals from the World Cup to his name. He then moved into coaching until 2012.

Northern Ireland

Considering some of the players who have played for Northern Ireland over the years – including Danny Blanchflower, Martin O'Neill, Norman Whiteside, and of course George Best – it is perhaps just a little surprising that the province has not enjoyed more World Cup success.

Northern Ireland's World Cup finest hour came during their first ever campaign in Sweden in 1958. In the first round group games they beat Czechoslovakia 1-0, lost 3-1 to Argentina and then drew 2-2 with West Germany, Peter McParland scoring both goals and 'keeper Harry Gregg putting in a brilliant performance. A play-off ensued, in which the Irish this time beat the Czechs 2-1 in extra time, the goals again coming from McParland. This result was all the more remarkable, because Czechoslovakia had previously beaten Argentina 6-1.

The quarter-final against France was a disappointment. Gregg was missing due to injury, and the team went down 4-0. Northern Ireland reached the Group D quarter-finals in 1982, where they again lost to France, this time by four goals to one. In 1986 they again qualified but went out at the group stage, drawing 1-1 with Algeria and losing 2-1 to Spain and 3-0 to Brazil. In their game against Brazil, Pat Jennings won his 119th cap.

Above: *Harry Gregg, Northern Ireland's goalkeeper, fails to stop West Germany's Uwe Seeler scoring during their World Cup match in 1958*

Officials

Referees have occasionally made headlines in World Cup matches, usually for the wrong reasons. Welsh referee Clive Thomas, for instance, became notorious for his strict timekeeping in 1978 in the Brazil v Sweden encounter. The match official allowed Brazil to take a second-half injury-time corner kick but blew for fulltime as Zico headed the dead-ball kick into the Swedish net. Thomas disallowed the goal and the match finished 1-1.

Another British referee, Jack Taylor, stood firm in the very first minute of the 1974 Final. The Dutch, and their total football, denied West Germany a touch of the ball, even as Johan Cruyff was challenged in the area by Uli Hoeness. Penalty! Johan Neeskens netted the spot kick. No-nonsense Taylor remained in charge and awarded a second penalty

when Bernd Hölzenbein was felled by Win Jansen. Paul Breitner levelled from the spot and the Germans recovered to win 2-1. Not all referees are eagle-eyed, however – the inexperienced Ali Ben Naceur was possibly the only man in Mexico City who saw nothing wrong as Maradona apparently out-jumped Peter Shilton in the Argentina v England quarterfinal clash. The squat midfielder's 'Hand of God' goal is now a part of World Cup folklore.

Even more obvious was German 'keeper Harald Schumacher's assault on France's Patrick Battiston. The Frenchman was clean through in the 1982 semi-final when the keeper dashed out of his area and smashed into Battista's face, leaving him unconscious and with a broken jaw that needed months of recovery time. Dutch referee Charles

Carver did not punish the German and even restarted play with a goal kick. And what of Geoff Hurst's infamous second goal in the 1966 Final? Did it cross the line? Swiss referee Gottfried Deist seemed undecided... but Russian linesman Tofik Bakhramov signalled a goal.

Russian referee Miroslav Stupor was at the centre of a bizarre incident in the 1982 encounter between France and Kuwait. The French were 3-1 up when Alain Giresse blasted in a fourth goal with the Kuwaiti back-line rooted to the spot. Apparently they thought they'd heard a whistle. It was enough for the Kuwaiti FA

president Prince Fahid to march onto the pitch to state his case. Amazingly, Stupor disallowed the goal.

Dubious decisions surface in any sport from time to time, but Spain had cause to complain about Gamal Ghandour's handling of their quarterfinal contest against South Korea in 2002. The Spaniard's had two goals ruled out against the co-hosts: the first, chalked off for supposed pushing looked decidedly 'iffy' but the second, disallowed for the ball going out of play according to the assistant referee, was an obvious error. The Koreans went on to win on penalties.

Oldest and Youngest

Below: *The Germany team of 1998*

The legendary Pelé is the youngest player to score in the World Cup Finals – he was 17 years and 39 days old when he scored for Brazil and Wales in the 1958 quarter-finals. Two matches later Pelé became the youngest World Cup winner, netting twice as Brazil

beat Sweden 5-2. Pelé lost his 'youngest player' tag when Norman Whiteside played – and was booked – for Northern Ireland against Yugoslavia in 1982, aged 17 years and 42 days. The youngest player to be sent off was Cameroon's Rigobert Song, dismissed at 17 years and 358 days against Brazil at USA '94. The oldest player to be dismissed also came at USA '94, and also against Brazil – Fernando Clavijo of USA was 37. Oldest player to strut his stuff on the World Cup stage was Cameroon's Roger Milla – he was 42 years and 39 days old when he played – and scored – against Russia in 1994. The oldest World Cup winner was Dino Zoff, Italian goalkeeper and captain, who was 40 when he lifted the cup in 1982.

The youngest World Cup referee was Uruguayan Francisco Mateuccia who was 27 years and 62 days when he officiated the Yugoslavia v Bolivia game in 1930. The oldest ref was England's George Reader who was 53 years and 236 days old when he took charge of the 1950 Brazil v Uruguay final. The oldest World Cup team was Germany against Iran in 1998, the average age being 31 years and 345 days. For the record, the highly experienced Germans won 2-0.

Above: *Antonio Carbajal, in training for the Mexican squad*

Only Players to Have...

The only player to have scored in successive World Cup Finals is Edvaldo Izidio Neto, better known as Vava, of Brazil, who scored twice in 1958 against Sweden and once in 1962 against Czechoslovakia. Both finals were won.

The only player to have scored five goals in a World Cup Finals match is Salenko of Russia in their 6-1 win over Cameroon in 1994. Despite his efforts, Russia was eliminated from the group stages.

The only player to have scored a hat-trick in a World Cup Final is Geoff Hurst (now Sir Geoff) of England, who netted three against West Germany in 1966. Despite the controversy that rages to this day over his second goal – did it cross the line or not? – it is always overlooked that he scored the perfect hat-trick, with a header, a right-foot shot and a left-foot shot.

The only player to have appeared in five World Cup Final tournaments is Antonio Carbajal of Mexico, who kept goal for his country in 1950, 1954, 1958, 1962 and 1966, making a total of 11 appearances.

The only manager to date to have led a country to two successes in the World Cup is Vittorio Pozzo of Italy, who succeeded in 1934 and 1938.

Owen

Born in Chester on 14 December 1979, Michael was spotted by Liverpool while playing schools football in Hawarden and signed as an apprentice, even though he had supported rivals Everton as a youngster! A member of the team that won the FA Youth Cup in 1996, he made the step up to the first team in May 1997, coming on as a substitute against Wimbledon and scoring.

The following season he was a first team regular and finished joint top scorer in the FA Premier League, his prowess in front of goal being noted by England manager Glenn Hoddle, who awarded him his first cap against Chile in February 1998. He thus became the youngest player to have represented his country all century.

It was at the World Cup that Owen made his name, coming on as a substitute in both the initial group matches and scoring and hitting a post against

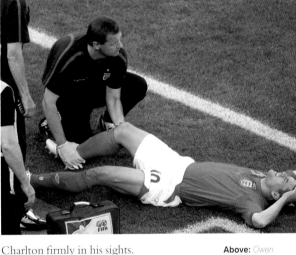

Romania. Calls for him to start a match grew. His sensational goal against

Argentina in the second round, running almost the length of the field and evading a number of tackles, confirmed his arrival on the world stage. Further strong performances at the 2000 and 2004 European Championships and 2002 World Cup, scoring in all three tournaments, marked him out as a striker of real quality and he is currently England's fourth best goalscorer, with Jimmy Greaves, Gary Lineker and Bobby

Charlton firmly in his sights.

After leaving Liverpool for Real Madrid in 2004, Owen had a disastrous 2006 World Cup picking up a serious knee injury which saw him return home and despite some sporadic appearances since then it is looking increasingly likely that his illustrious international career may be drawing to a close. Inconsistent form at Newcastle saw him overlooked for England selection for the 2010 tournament. He now carves out a career in the media.

Above: Owen is treated on the pitch after badly injuring his right knee playing for England against Sweden in the 2006 tournament

Pelé

The teenage Pelé made a spectacular entry to World Cup football with Brazil in 1958 – and will be the face of their 2014 campaign. Brazil went on to win the tournament in Sweden; Pelé went on to become the greatest player in the game. His blend of power, wonderful technique and flair made him virtually impossible to pin down – legally that is. He suffered brutal treatment in the 1966 tournament and famously left the finals injured and in tears. But he wept tears of joy in 1958 after Brazil beat the host nation 5-2 in the Final.

Pelé chipped in with two goals, one a breath-taking effort – trapping the ball on his thigh in a crowded penalty area, hooking it over his head and then volleying past goalkeeper Svensson. The 17 year-old prodigy, full name Edson Arantes do Nascimento, and with a semi-final hat-trick against France already under his belt, was the youngest World Cup winner, and there was plenty more to follow. Brazil won the trophy again in 1962, although Pelé's involvement was minimal after picking up an injury in the early stages. Four years later Bulgarian and Portuguese defenders kicked him out of the 1966 competition in England and he was a forlorn figure as Brazil limped out following the group matches. At the time he vowed never to appear in another World Cup. Fortunately for Brazil and football lovers across the globe he had changed his mind by 1970.

Brazil's squad simply oozed class and, of course, they had Pelé, now aged 29 and in his footballing prime. To no one's

surprise they made it through to another Final – but only after they survived a titanic tussle against England in Group 3. Worthy of the Final itself, the contest served up two iconic moments. The first came as early as the tenth minute when Pelé rose to meet a Jairzinho cross with a textbook, full-blooded header. Miraculously Gordon Banks thwarted the master striker by getting down to make what many consider the save of the century. A single Jairzinho strike – laid on by Pelé – settled the encounter after which Pelé and England captain Bobby Moore were seen by the world smiling, embracing and swapping shirts, each recognising that the other was a master of his trade.

Italy were brushed aside 4-1 in the Final as Brazil performed on a different level. Fittingly Pelé netted the third goal – Brazil's 100th World Cup goal – as his country claimed the trophy for the third time, and Pelé his third winners' medal. Tarciscio Burgnich, the Italian defender assigned to mark the Brazilian Number 10, said: "I told myself before the game, he's made of skin and bones just like everyone else, but I was wrong."

Above: *Legends appreciation society, Pelé and Bobby Moore exchange shirts, 1970*

Penalty Shoot-outs

Penalty shoot-outs were first introduced at the 1970 Watney Cup Final between Hull City and Manchester United (George Best was the first player to take one, and Denis Law the first to miss) and have since become an integral part of the World Cup.

The first World Cup finals match to be decided on a penalty shootout was the West Germany and France semi-final in 1982, with the Germans winning 5-4. Since then there has been at least two matches requiring a penalty shoot-out at every World Cup, with four in 1990 being the record. That year included both semi-finals, as Argentina (against Italy) and West Germany (against England) won 4-3 to reach the Final.

Not surprisingly, Germany and Argentina top the table of the most successful nations in penalty shoot-outs, having won all three they have been involved in. At the other end of the table comes Italy, who lost all three of theirs, including the 1994 Final against Brazil, until reversing that record in 2006 with a 5-3 triumph over France in the 2006 final.

While there are 13 players who have scored in two separate shoot-outs, no player has scored in three. The closest is Roberto Baggio, who scored in penalty shoot-outs against Argentina (in 1990) and France (in 1998) but missed the decisive penalty against Brazil in the Final of 1994.

Pickles

The tale of Pickles the dog has gone down in World Cup history. The Jules Rimet Trophy was stolen from an exhibition prior to the 1966 World Cup in England, and goldsmiths and silversmiths all over the country rubbed their hands of making an emergency replacement in time for the tournament. They were, however, to be thwarted by a small dog.

Pickles' owner, one David Corbett, was being taken for a walk by his dog in suburban south London, when he was suddenly pulled towards a hedge. Beneath this hedge, Pickles had sniffed out a metal object wrapped in newspaper. It was the World Cup.

Mr. Corbett could hardly believe his eyes as he unwrapped the cup. He said at the time that he knew it was the trophy when he saw the words Germany, Uruguay and Brazil engraved upon it. That was of course something of a giveaway, so Pickles' and his owner immediately scampered towards the nearest police station. The world of football was suitably grateful to the two year-old Pickles, and a reward of

£3,000 was paid to Mr Corbett. It is to be hoped that Pickles got something out of it too.

Above: *Pickles the dog with owner David Corbett*

Platini

Michel Platini's midfield artistry helped France become a real footballing force in the 1980s and his skills and influence were key factors in no fewer than three World Cup campaigns.

Platini made his name with French League side Nancy and scored on his international debut against Czechoslovakia in 1976. France were drawn in a tough group in the 1978 finals. Italy beat them 2-1 and Argentina won by the same score line – but it might have been different had the French taken a number of chances created by

Platini, who had scored his first World Cup goal to level matters. France were eliminated, despite beating Hungary 3-1.

The French harboured genuine hopes of doing well in Spain; their midfield, featuring Jean Tigana and Alain Giresse alongside team captain Platini, sparkled throughout. The semi-final clash with arch rivals West Germany was a classic. The pulsating contest ended 3-3 and featured a man-of-the-match display by Platini – but France were edged out on penalties.

Platini earned a high-profile move to Juventus after leading France to success in the 1984 European Championship, in which he was outstanding, and he starred for his country once again in the 1986 World Cup finals, scoring against Italy with an elegant chip and with a simple side-footer against Brazil. But as in Spain, the French were beaten in the last four by the West Germans, this time by 2-0.

Left: *The Polish World Cup team, 2002*

Poland

Poland arrived at the 2002 World Cup with high expectations after an impressive qualifying campaign after an absence of 16 years. Unfortunately, the team failed to live up to their pre-tournament hype and lost their opening match against hosts and eventual semi-finalists South Korea. Another reversal, this time against much-fancied Portugal, preceded a consolation victory against Russia that was not enough to see them progress to the second phase. The Poles' first World Cup outing in 1938 also proved to be a first-round exit, when they failed to overcome Brazil in an extraordinary encounter which the South Americans won 6-5 after extra-time despite Ernst Wilimoski scoring four goals.

Perhaps their most famous World Cup performance in English eyes came at Wembley in October 1973 when the heroics of keeper Jan Tomaszewski secured the draw that took Poland to the '74 finals for the first time in 36 years and ended Sir Alf Ramsey's days as England manager. Their performance in West Germany was rewarded with victory in the third-place play-off against Brazil. Brazil would again halt the Poles' progress in 1978 and 1986 after they had successfully negotiated the first round. The 1982 tournament in Spain saw Poland lose to eventual winners Italy in the semis but they repeated their third-place finish of 1974 with a 3-2 victory over France.

Portugal

Portugal burst onto the World Cup scene in 1966, the first time they had succeeded in qualifying for the tournament finals after seven attempts. Their 'Black Pearl', Eusebio, finished top scorer with nine goals which helped his country clinch third place in England. Impressive first round victories over Hungary (3-0), Bulgaria (3-0) and holders Brazil (3-1) saw them cruise through to a quarter-final meeting with North Korea. Trailing 0-3, the dream looked over until a Eusebio hat-trick inspired a comeback and an eventual 5-3 victory. They were unable to overcome hosts and eventual winners England in the semi-final, but clinched third place with a 2-1 victory over Russia.

It would be 20 years before Portugal again qualified but, despite beating England 1-0 in their opening match, defeats against Poland and Morocco saw them packing their bags after the first round. Portugal contested only their third World Cup finals in 2002 but they endured mixed fortunes on the field. Having lost their first match against the United States, a 4-0 victory over Poland gave their supporters false hope as a single-goal reversal against hosts South Korea again saw the team enjoying more of a summer holiday than they had initially hoped for. Beaten by France at the last four stage in Germany 2006, Portugal were disappointed not to make the World Cup Final.

Puskas

The 'Galloping Major' was captain of the wonderful Hungarian side that lost just one game between 1950 and 1956. That one game, unfortunately, was the 1954 World Cup Final against West Germany. Ferenc Puskas, though, remains one of the best players of all time. Considered weak in the air and totally left-footed, he was a magician on the ball – especially for the 'Magical Magyars' for whom he scored 83 goals in 84 games, an international record bettered only by Pelé. Puskas captained the Hungarian team that bamboozled England 6-3 at Wembley in 1953 – and he scored four times as Real Madrid overwhelmed Eintracht Frankfurt 7-3 in the 1960 European Cup Final.

Hungary were the clear favourites at the 1954 World Cup finals in Switzerland, and once they had trounced Korea, 9-0, and West Germany, 8-3, in the opening two games they looked unstoppable. But an ankle injury to Puskas in that second game kept him out until the Final.

He declared himself fit and the gamble looked a good one as the Hungarians went two-up only for the Germans to hit back with three goals of their own. When Puskas returned to the finals in Chile eight years later it was for Spain – he qualified on residency grounds – but his new country were eliminated after the group stage. The great Puskas died on November 17, 2006.

Above: *Puskas, captain of the 'Magic Magyars' Hungarian team*

Qualifying Matches

Below: *Top scorer*
Archie Thompson
of Australia

The very first World Cup to require a qualifying competition was in 1934 in Italy, for 32 countries wished to participate in a competition that could only accommodate 16. Even the hosts were expected to qualify, being handed a fixture against Greece which they duly won 4-0.

Although it was intended to play qualifying matches on a home and away basis, it was not always possible – Greece withdrew after they had lost the first leg to Italy, Bulgaria similarly withdrew midway through their group matches, with Austria and Hungary being handed places in the finals and France v Germany was never played because both countries had already qualified by beating Luxembourg. Over the years the qualifying competition has become more refined, although it has not been without its problems, with the Soviet Union refusing to play a play-off match in Chile for political reasons and being expelled from the 1974 competition and Haiti and El Salvador going to war after El Salvador won a play-off for a place in the 1970 finals.

The record score in a World Cup qualifying match was achieved in the Oceania group, with Australia beating American Samoa 31-0, with Archie Thompson scoring 13 of the goals, itself a record. The score was originally reported as being 32-0, the scorekeepers having lost count. And in the following four years, Thompson scored only four more goals for his country.

Quickest...

The quickest goal in a World Cup finals match was scored after 11 second's by Hakan Sukur of Turkey. This was against South Korea in 2002, in the third and fourth place play-off, Turkey going on to win 3-2.

The quickest hat-trick in the World Cup finals was registered by Laszlo Kiss of Hungary against El Salvador in 1982. He scored in the 70th, 74th and 77th minutes after coming on as a substitute, the only substitute to have netted a hat trick. Ebbe Sand of Denmark scored the quickest goal by a substitute, netting 16 seconds after coming on against Nigeria in 1998.

The quickest dismissal during a World Cup finals came after 56 seconds of the match between Uruguay and Scotland in 1986, with Jose Batista being the unfortunate player to be sent off.

The quickest return home following a World Cup tournament would probably be a toss-up between Brazil and Argentina. Both countries were drawn in qualifying groups with one other country – Brazil with Peru in Group 2 and Argentina with Chile in Group 3. Both Chile and Peru withdrew from the competition before qualifying matches could be played, so both Brazil and Argentina headed off to the 1934 Finals in Italy. There they both lost their ties in the preliminary round, Brazil 3-1 against Spain and Argentina 3-2 against Sweden, and promptly headed back home across the Atlantic.

Below: *Ebbe Sand of Denmark celebrates his goal seconds after coming on as a sub, 1998*

Ramsey

Below: *Alf Ramsey and Bobby Moore show off the World Cup, 1966*

Alfred Ernest Ramsey, born in Dagenham in 1920, was a very accomplished full-back who played for Southampton and Tottenham. He made 32 appearances for England, three of them as captain. As a manager he guided Ipswich Town to the First Division championship and then, in 1963, he was put in charge of the England team.

Alf Ramsey predicted that his side would win the World Cup in 1966. He made meticulous preparations for the tournament and a lot of people thought that he, and his tactics, were extremely boring. Perhaps they were – but they worked, and Ramsey's Wingless Wonders duly became champions of the world.

Ramsey seemed dull and uninspiring to many, but he actually had excellent motivational skills to accompany his mature footballing brain. When the 1966 Final went into extra time, he gathered his players together and famously said: "You've won it once. Now you'll have to go out there and win it again". And of course they did.

Ramsey became Sir Alf in 1970, but his cautious tactics were blamed for England's defeat by West Germany in that year's World Cup. When England failed to qualify in 1974, he was sacked. Sir Alf Ramsey died in 1999.

Rimet

Jules Rimet, born in 1873, was president of the French Football Association from 1919 until 1945, and president of FIFA from 1921 until 1954. He is credited with the creation of the World Cup competition, and he was certainly its principal instigator.

The first World Cup trophy was eventually named in honour of Monsieur Rimet. It was gold-plated silver, and it stood 35cm high and weighed 3.8kg. The cup had an eventful existence. In order to keep it from the clutches of the Nazis, it was placed in a shoebox and hidden under a bed in Italy during the Second World War. It was stolen in 1966 and rescued by Pickles the dog, and then it was stolen again in 1983. The second theft occurred in Brazil, and as Brazilian dogs are more interested in sniffing out food scraps than World Cups, it was never recovered. The Jules Rimet Trophy was probably melted down and Brazil, who held the trophy in perpetuity as they had won it for the third time in 1970, now had to make do with a replica.

Jules Rimet himself died in 1956. He had certainly started something.

Below: *Jules Rimet, president of FIFA, presents the first World Cup trophy to Dr Paul Jude, the president of the Uruguayan Football Association, 1930*

Right: *The bleached blonde Romanians line up before their game against Tunisia in the 1998 World Cup*

Romania

One of the four European nations (along with France, Belgium and Yugoslavia) that took part in the inaugural World Cup, Romania travelled to South America with a team 'managed' by their King. He threatened the British oil company that employed most of the country's leading footballers with closure unless his chosen players were given paid leave to attend the tournament. His charges beat Peru before making a first-round exit to hosts and eventual winners Uruguay.

They fared little better in their next two outings, losing to Czechoslovakia in 1934 and Cuba in 1938 after extra-time and a replay. It wasn't until 1970 that Romania again managed to qualify but they failed to progress past the first round. Italia '90 saw them contest the second round for the first time, but they lost their penalty shootout against the Republic of Ireland. The USA-hosted 1994 tournament was the scene of the nation's greatest World Cup performance where a Gheorghe Hagi-inspired team again lost out on penalties, this time at the quarter-final stage to Sweden, after an impressive 3-2 victory over Argentina in the previous round.

Romania couldn't overcome Croatia in a second-round tie four years later and failed to qualify for both the 2002 and 2006 tournaments.

Ronaldo

Respected in the same manner as Pelé, Ronaldo was the undoubted star of the 2002 World Cup as Brazil claimed an unprecedented fifth title. He scored in each match of the group stage, against Turkey, China and Costa Rica, and then against Belgium in the second round before drawing a blank against England in the quarter-final. The semi-final brought another goal against Turkey and lined up Germany as their Final opponents. He scored the only two goals of the game to take his tally to eight and earn the Golden Boot as the tournament's highest goalscorer.

These rewards more than made amends for his previous World Cup Final appearance in 1998. An uninspired Brazilian team had struggled through the first round, beating Morocco 3-0 but relying on an own goal to beat Scotland and then losing to Norway. Chile were summarily dispatched 4-1 in the second round with Ronaldo scoring twice. He was also on target in the semi-final against Holland, but it took a penalty shoot-out to eliminate the Dutch. He was widely criticised for his performance in the Final as the French hosts ran out 3-0 winners but it was later reported that Ronaldo had suffered some sort of fit the night before and many questioned his ability to cope with the pressures of such a big game.

Awarded the accolade of FIFA Player of the Year in 1996, 1997 and 2002, Ronaldo had also been part of the Brazilian side that had returned triumphant from America in 1994 but had not made an appearance. Born in Bento Ribeiro in 1976, Ronaldo Luiz Naz came to the attention of former World Cup winner Jairzinho as a 14 year-old and he signed professional with Cruzeiro Esporte Clube as soon as he was old enough. He moved to PSV Eindhoven in 1994 before joining Barcelona in 1996, where many argue he had his finest season. A transfer to Inter Milan followed in 1997 although his career at the San Siro was afflicted by knee injuries. He regained his form and could not resist the lure of Real Madrid in 2002, where he has since plied his trade with some of the current game's greatest names in Raul, Luis Figo, Roberto Carlos and David Beckham.

Ronaldo scored his 15th World Cup goal against Ghana in Germany 2006 and overtook Müller to become the highest goalscorer in World Cup despite Brazil being beaten by France in the quarter-finals.

Rooney

Fast and powerful, with good body strength and a vicious shot with either foot, Wayne Rooney emerged during the 2004 European Championships in much the same way that his then city rival Michael Owen had emerged in 1998.

Born in Liverpool on 24 October 1985, Wayne has set records at every step of the game. The youngest goalscorer in the history of the Premiership when netting for Everton at the age of 16 years 360 days (a record subsequently beaten, and Wayne no longer holds even the Everton record), he went on to become England's youngest ever international player when making his debut against Australia in February 2003. He then became the country's youngest goalscorer and extended that record to become the youngest scorer in the history of the European Championships when netting against Switzerland (a Swiss player subsequently took that record from him too).

With Rooney's enthusiasm and power, coupled with Michael Owen's rediscovered goal form, there were real

hopes that England might go on to lift the 2004 European Championship, but a broken foot, sustained in the eventual defeat by Portugal put paid to England's chances and Rooney's career for a number of months. By the time he returned to the game he had been transferred from Everton to Manchester United in a deal that was potentially worth £27 million, depending on appearances. When Rooney is in full flight, scoring goals with regularity, his fee and current wages of £300,000 a week look value for money. However, if a player is to be defined by their performance on the major stage then his 2014 campaign will have to be sensational. Up until Brazil, he had failed to score in eight frustrating World Cup matches.

Rossi

Although he scored three times during Italy's campaign in Argentina in 1978 and was a squad member in Mexico in 1986, it was as top-scorer in the 1982 tournament that Juventus striker Paolo Rossi made his name. The 25 year-old Rossi was fortunate to even be in the Italian squad, having returned from a two-year match-fixing ban the previous April. The alleged incident, which Rossi continually denied, took place while he was on loan with Perugia and it was while he was banned that Juventus paid Serie B club Lanerossi Vicenza a bargain £500,000 for his services.

Italy scraped through the first round with a better goal difference than Cameroon. The second phase saw them pitted against the South American might of Argentina and Brazil and Rossi was given an ultimatum to score in the latter game, having failed to previously find the net. He did not disappoint, notching a hat-trick as Brazil were dispatched 3-2 to set up a semi-final clash with Poland. Pablito, as he was dubbed after the 1978 tournament, scored both goals in the 2-0 victory that secured their place in the Final.

It was Rossi who sent the Italian fans into raptures as he scored the first as Italy triumphed 3-1 over West Germany to secure their third title.

Russia

The USSR did not participate in the first five World Cup tournaments for political reasons. Their first three campaigns illustrated that the golden era of Russian football was the 1950s and 1960s, reaching the quarter-final at their first attempt in 1958. Having triumphed in a first round play-off against England, the Soviets fell to hosts Sweden in the last eight. Four years later, they again failed to make it past the quarter-finals, losing to the hosts once more, this time Chile. They went one better in England in 1966 when they won all their group games (against North Korea, Italy and Chile) before putting out Hungary in the quarterfinal. They lost to eventual runners-up West Germany in the semi-final and could not prevent Portugal from claiming third in the play-off.

The 1970 tournament, where they lost to Uruguay at the quarter-final stage, would prove the last time they qualified until Spain in 1982. There, and in Mexico four years later, the Soviets failed to make it past the second stage in their last outings as the USSR. Since 1992, with the demise of the Soviet Union, Russia has failed to make it past the first round, failing to qualify for the last two Finals. Lucky then, they are hosts in 2018.

Scandals

Scandals are nothing new to the World Cup; they have been around as long the competition. In 1930 hosts Uruguay left nothing to chance in preparing their players for the tournament ahead, with the entire squad being shut away for training and confined to a hotel in Montevideo for almost eight weeks before the competition kicked off. Goalkeeper Antonio Mazzali had been a member of Uruguay's winning Olympic sides of 1924 and 1928 and was first choice in what was a strongly fancied host nation. Uruguay ultimately won the competition, but they did so without Mazzali; he sneaked out of the hotel one night to see his family, was caught upon his return and promptly sent home for good.

There were plenty of scandals surrounding the Mexico World Cup in 1970, most of them involving England, the holders. The problems began almost as soon as England arrived on the South American continent to acclimatise themselves, with Bobby Moore being arrested on suspicion of stealing a gold bracelet from a shop in Colombia, but the whole episode had more than a hint of 'fit-up' surrounding it; Bobby Charlton was supposed to have been the decoy who distracted the shop assistant while Moore pocketed the bracelet!

It was, however, merely a taste of what was to come for England when they arrived in Mexico; local supporters camped outside the team hotel and banged drums and blew horns all night to prevent the team from sleeping, even more so when England were due to play Brazil. Add to this the mysterious stomach upset that

only affected goalkeeper Gordon Banks, widely held to be the world number one, and it is easy to see why England believed they were deliberately targeted.

While drug taking or the use of banned substances had been a problem for athletics for many years, football had survived relatively unscathed until 1974, when Haitian Ernest Jean-Joseph was banned by FIFA. His manager refused to have him sent home and it took security officials flown in from Haiti to get him extradited. The following tournament saw Scotland's Willie Johnston sent home after he was caught taking an illegal drug, supposedly for medicinal purposes. But it was in 1994 that the World Cup captured its most famous miscreant; Diego Maradona, a winner in 1986 and runner-up in 1990 was caught after the 4-0 win over Greece in Argentina's opening match. Argentina's fighting spirit seemed to accompany him on the plane back home, for although

they beat Nigeria 2-1 they never hit the heights again and were knocked out in the second round.

There have always been accusations that fortune doesn't always favour the brave, it usually favours the home side. Certainly there were one or two eyebrows raised during the 2002 competition when Japan and (particularly) South Korea seemed to get a more than lenient hand when it came to refereeing decisions. But surely this was nothing on an incident just prior to the kick-off of the 1930 World Cup Final between Uruguay and Argentina. Both sides insisted on using a ball manufactured in their own country, with Uruguay as hosts doubly insistent that it was their right. In the end the referee came up with a compromise; an Argentinean ball was used in the first half and at half time (with Argentina leading 2-1) the ball was swapped for a Uruguayan ball. The Uruguayans netted three times in the second half to win the trophy.

Scotland

Like the other British national teams, Scotland did not enter the World Cup until 1950 when, differences with FIFA settled, the Home Internationals doubled as a qualifying group with first and second to go through. Scotland declared that they would only travel to Brazil as champions. A 1-0 defeat by England at Hampden Park condemned them to second place and summer at home.

The first of eight successful qualification campaigns came in 1954 but an ill-prepared 13-man squad was humbled 7-0 by Uruguay. The Scots fared only slightly better in Sweden in 1958. Heroics in 1974 included a 0-0 draw with reigning champions Brazil but came to naught as Willie Ormond's men were eliminated on goal difference in a three-way tie without losing a game.

Hopes were high in 1978 but a 3-2 victory over eventual Finalists Holland was insufficient to make up for poor showings against Peru and Iran. Ally McLeod's ageing team lost out on goal difference, which proved decisive again four years later. After three further tournaments – 1986, 1990 and 1998 – the Scots have yet to progress beyond the initial phase.

Off the pitch, Scotland's travelling supporters, the Tartan Army, are regarded as amongst the best in the world. Gordon Strachan was appointed manager in January 2013, after Craig Levein was sacked, but two opening defeats in qualifying meant that Scotland were the first UEFA team to be eliminated for the 2014 Finals.

Shock Results

The 2002 World Cup finals threw up a number of shock results – right from the opening fixture of the tournament, when France, the World and European Champions, were humbled by World Cup debutants Senegal. El Hadji Diouf repeatedly harassed the French defence but it was Papa Bouba Diop who netted the conclusive goal after 30 minutes. Co-hosts South Korea also rocked the establishment, first overcoming Portugal at the group stage then securing a surprise 2-1 golden goal win over Italy.

The tournament has enjoyed a number of shock results over the years – none more surprising than England's single-goal loss to the USA in 1950. England considered themselves invincible at the time and fielded the likes of Tom Finney, Stan Mortensen, Billy Wright, Alf Ramsey and Wilf Mannion. The American side were, as expected, pinned back in their half in the first 30 minutes in Belo Horizonte but, eight minutes before the break the USA broke clear and Joe Gaetjens netted what proved to be the winning goal. The pre-tournament favourites had been knocked out by the rank outsiders.

Above: *Omam Biyik of Cameroon scores during the 1990 World Cup against Argentina*

that five.

Rabah Madjer put the Algerians ahead after 54 minutes and, although Karl-Heinz Rummenigge levelled after 68 minutes, Lakhdar Belloumi responded immediately to secure a famous win. The unfancied Algerians would have qualified for the latter stages had the Germans and Austria not played out a contrived result (1-0). Also in 1982 Northern Ireland grabbed a shock win against the host nation, Spain. What's more they did so with only 10 men, Mal Donaghy having been sent off on the hour. Gerry Armstrong's 47th-minute strike settled the outcome.

For incident, drama and excitement, Cameroon's stunning win over defending champions Argentina at the San Siro Stadium in 1990 made gripping viewing. Cameroon were down to ten men in the 61st minute, Andre Kana-Biyick being red carded for a rugged foul on Claudio Caniggia, but they went ahead six minutes later through Francois Omam-Biyick. Argentina, Maradona and all, couldn't respond, not even when Benjamin Massing was dismissed in the closing stages. Nine-man Cameroon held out for one of the all-time shock World Cup victories.

Close on the heels of that shock, though, came North Korea's 1-0 win over Italy at Middlesborough's Ayrsome Park – a result that sent the Italians home to a barrage of rotten tomatoes. Another shock looked likely as the Koreans raced into a 3-0 lead over Portugal in the quarter-finals but four-goal Eusebio inspired his side to a 5-3 victory. Algeria v West Germany in 1982 looked a one-horse race. The Africans were 1000-1 to win the cup, while the Germans had lost a mere four matches in four years. Make

Spain

Spain were perennial underachievers until they finally won the World Cup in 2010, with a team packed with stars.

Spain manager Vicente del Bosque managed to raise his players from an opening defeat as they became the eighth team to win the World Cup, with a tight, if ill-tempered, 1-0 win over the Netherlands. Andrés Iniesta scored the winner, while 14 yellow and one red card were handed out.

Spain had long confounded their fanatical supporters with early World Cup exits prior to 2010. Their first entry saw a 3-1 first round victory over Brazil in 1934 take them to the quarter-final where they succumbed to Italy after extra-time and a replay. Their second appearance resulted in a semi-final loss against Brazil and defeat in the third place play-off against Sweden in 1950. It would be more than 30 years before Spain graced the second round of the competition.

Much was expected of the 1982 hosts, but the opening 1-1 draw with Honduras set the tone for the campaign as Spain won just one of their group matches on their way to the second phase.

Sweden

Finishing runners-up as hosts in the 1958 Final, losing out to a Pelé inspired Brazil, remains the pinnacle of Sweden's World Cup achievements. First round victories over Mexico and Hungary in '58 were accompanied by a goal-less draw with Wales. They defeated the USSR in the quarter-final and overcame defending champions West Germany in the semi. They scored first in the Final to leave the Brazilians trailing for the only time in the tournament, but eventually succumbed 5-2, with 17 year-old Pelé grabbing a brace.

It was not the only time that Sweden impressed in the final stages, however: they have been losing semi-finalists on three occasions. In 1938 they were thrashed 5-1 by Hungary after seeing off Cuba 8-0 in the quarter-final, having been handed a walkover in the first round when Austria withdrew, only to lose the third-place play-off against Brazil. Third-place finishes followed in 1950, when defeats against Brazil and Uruguay preceded a play-off victory over Spain, and 1994, losing to Brazil in the semi-final before beating Bulgaria in the play-off. First-round exits in 1970, 1978 and 1990 and a second-round golden goal defeat at the hands of Senegal suggest Sweden have the potential but not the consistency to dominate world football.

Tardelli

There is little in the game that Marco Tardelli did not achieve during a long and illustrious career; winner's medals in the UEFA Cup Winners and European Cups, five times a League champion and twice an Italian Cup winner are among the honours achieved with Juventus, but it is for his goal in the 1982 World Cup Final playing for Italy against West Germany that Marco probably derived the most pleasure.

Born in Capanne di Careggine on 24 September 1954, he played for Pisa and Como before getting a move to Juventus in 1975. He had an immediate impact at Juve, earning the first of his 81 caps against Portugal in 1976 as an aggressive midfield powerhouse, with a brief to sit in front of the defenders but make the occasional burst forward, which earned him the nickname Schizzo (meaning 'spurt').

A member of the Italian sides that finished fourth in both the 1978 World Cup and 1980 European Championships, it was in the 1982 World Cup that the Italians in general and Tardelli in particular came into their own, eliminating the holders Argentina and favourites Brazil in the second group phase to set up a majestic route to the Final. Tardelli wore down the German midfield, helping to set up two goals and netting the other himself as Italy won 3-1, one of only six goals he scored for his country.

He left Juventus after the 1985 European Cup, won against the backdrop of the Heysel disaster, and signed with Inter, but his best days were behind him. He collected his final cap for Italy in September 1985 and retired from playing in 1988, subsequently taking his coaching badge. Marked out as a future Italian manager, Marco has yet to make a real impact at management level, and left his role as Republic of Ireland assistant manager in 2013 after five years.

Two-Timers

Only a few players have represented more than one country at the finals – and recent rule changes mean this will no longer happen. First person to do so was centre-half Luis Monti, who made it to consecutive finals with Argentina and Italy. In 1930 Monti helped Argentina into the Final with the only goal of the game against France and then scoring in the first half against the United States in the semis.

After the break the Argentineans went goal-happy, running out 6-1 winners, but they were beaten by Uruguay 4-2 in the Final. By 1934 Monti was representing Italy and this time he picked up a winners' medal as the Italians came from behind to defeat Czechoslovakia 2-1 in Rome.

The legendary schemer Ferenc Puskas played for Hungary in 1954 and Spain in 1962 – as did José Santamaria, who had played for Uruguay in 1954. José Altafini, also known as Mazzola, played for Brazil in 1958 and Italy in 1962.

Yugoslav pair Robert Prosinecki and Robert Jarni played for their homeland in 1990 but, with the break-up of that country, switched to Croatia in 1998. Prosinecki is a World Cup record breaker – he scored in Yugoslavia's 4-1 win over the United Arab Emirates in 1990 and then netted for Croatia in the 3-1 victory over Jamaica. That made him the first player to score for separate countries. The creative midfielder, who once played for Portsmouth, added another that year as Croatia took third place with a 2-1 over Holland.

Unusual

Not surprisingly given the number of matches played, there have been a number of unusual occurrences in the World Cup finals. Did you know, for example, that the Brazil v England game in 1962 had to be halted because a dog ran onto the pitch? Jimmy Greaves had to go down on all fours to catch it. More recently – in 1994 – Mexico and Bulgaria's second-round encounter was held up for 15 minutes because a crossbar broke. And what of the unusual Kiss? Hungary's Laszlo Kiss is the only substitute to score a hat-trick at the Finals: his side were 5-1 ahead against El Salvador in 1982 when he took the field and helped Hungary to a thumping 10-1 victory.

Detroit's Pontiac Silverdome hosted the 1-1 draw between USA and Switzerland in 1994 – unusual in

that it was the first time a World Cup match had been played indoors. In 1986, Argentina's Marcelo Trobbiani made his only World Cup appearance as an 88th minute substitute in the Final against West Germany – equalling the record for the shortest World Cup career set by Tunisia's Khemais Labidi in 1978. Red and yellow cards were introduced for the 1970 tournament – however, no one was dismissed that year. Denmark's Ebbe Sand made history in 1998 with the fastest goal by a substitute, scoring just 16 seconds after coming on in the 4-1 victory over Nigeria.

Above:
Switzerland and the USA entering Pontiac Silverdome stadium in the 1994 World Cup

Uruguay

Hosts of the inaugural World Cup in 1930, Uruguay became the first champions beating Argentina 4-2, after being 2-1 down at half-time, in a thrilling Final in the Centenario Stadium, Montevideo. In 1934, the Uruguayans declined to travel to Italy as a retaliatory gesture for the snubbing of their tournament by the Europeans and are the only holders not to have defended their title. Four years later, they withdrew again, this time in protest at FIFA's decision to stage a second successive competition in Europe.

The 1950 finals in Brazil were played in two group stages and lacked a scheduled Final. The climactic game between favourites Brazil and Uruguay became the de facto Final with the victors taking the trophy. In front of a world record crowd of 199,854 at the Maracana, Ivan Lopez's team sent the host nation into mourning with an unexpected 2-1 victory.

Fourth place in 1954 and 1970 remain the Uruguayans, best since. In 1966, Uruguay lost 4-0 to West Germany in the quarter-final and had two sent off. 1986 and 1990 saw them achieve the last 16 but in 1974 and 2002 they were eliminated at the group stage. In 2010, a handball on the goal-line by Luis Suarez prevented Ghana's Dominic Adiyiah from scoring in the last minute and Asamoah Gyan missed the penalty – with Uruguay triumphing in the shoot-out to make the semi-finals. They lost to the Dutch 3-2 in the third-place play-off.

USA

Having lost 12-2 on aggregate in two games against Mexico during the qualifying stages of the 1950 World Cup, the USA, to the astonishment of just about everyone, beat England 1-0 in a group game. This did not, however, herald the start of world domination in soccer by the Americans.

Enthusiasm for real football has waxed and waned in the United States since then, but by 1994 the country had pronounced itself ready and eager to host the World Cup. Four years earlier they had reached the final stages in Italy, although their results on that occasion were less than spectacular: in their group games the USA had lost 5-1 to Czechoslovakia, 1-0 to Italy, and 2-1 to Austria. In 1994, with automatic qualification, they hoped to do rather better. FIFA experienced one or two problems with the US authorities, who wanted bigger goals and penalty shootouts after every drawn game, but the tournament was nonetheless a success. They qualified for the second round by drawing 1-1 with Switzerland, beating Colombia 2-1 and losing to Romania by just a goal to nil. They were then perhaps a little unfortunate in being matched against Brazil, but again lost by only a single goal. They reached the last eight in 2010 and have a shrewd coach in Jurgen Klinsmann.

Valderrama

'El Pibe' (the kid) captained Colombia in three World Cups and with 111 appearances is his country's most capped player. His shock of frizzy hair and equally eye-catching midfield skills marked him apart from the rest. The charismatic Carlos Valderrama came from a footballing family – father was a defender and an uncle was a winger, while two more uncles, four cousins and two brothers were also professionals. He made his debut for Colombia in October 1985, against Paraguay, and was soon a regular.

Hugely influential, his World Cup highlight was mesmerising several West German players in 1990 before crossing perfectly for Fredy Rincon to score an all-important injury time equaliser to ensure qualification. During the qualifying stages for the 1994 competition Valderrama was at his peak and his sensational displays earned him a second South American Footballer of the Year award. He masterminded a 5-0 thrashing of Argentina en route to USA '94 and performed well in the finals but his team-mates failed to shine and one of the favourites slipped out at the group stage. Four years later, at 37, he was hardly a kid in France, but El Pibe still stood out as a playmaker, even if Colombia once again struggled.

Venues for 2014

The 2014 FIFA World Cup will be the 20th tournament and takes place between 12 June and 13 July in Brazil. It is the second time that Brazil has hosted the competition, after first holding the showpiece event in 1950.

Brazil was elected unchallenged in 2007 after FIFA decreed that the tournament would be staged in South America for the first time since Argentina 1978.

The official FIFA list for World Cup 2014 venues (18) is Belém, Belo Horizonte, Brasília, Campo Grande, Cuiabá, Curitiba, Florianópolis, Fortaleza, Goiânia, Maceió, Manaus,

FIFA WORLD CUP
Brasil

2013 and others far from being finished.

The opening match will take place at the Arena de São Paulo, while the most iconic city in Brazil also includes probably the most iconic stadium in world football. The Maracana was rebuilt purposefully for the World Cup. It officially reopened in June 2013, when Brazil hosted England in a 2-2 friendly draw. The stadium will host the final on July 13. The capacity is now 71, 159, the largest venue of the 18 cities. The smallest venue is the Arena da Baixada, with 37, 634.

Brazil is certainly using its vast expanse when it comes to venues. The Arena da Amazônia in Manuas, an Amazonas state, is not a traditional area for Brazilian football. There has been some speculation that it might be used as a prison after the World Cup to relieve overcrowding elsewhere. Due to its rainforest location, humidity can reach up to 99 per cent in June and July. Some 4,750kms south, the Jose Pinheiro Borda stadium in Port Alegre originally took 10 years to build, and was finally opened in 1969 with fans contributing the bricks. For the 2014 tournament, reconstruction has been plagued by financial issues.

Natal, Porto Alegre, Recife, Rio Branco, Rio de Janeiro, Salvador and São Paulo. A host of problems blighted the build-up, with three arenas missing FIFA's end-of-year deadline for completion in

Wales

The 1958 World Cup saw all four of the home countries qualify for the finals in Sweden, but Wales were lucky to scrape in. Along with Uruguay they were in fact eliminated in the preliminary round, but Israel's opponents had all withdrawn, and so Uruguay were offered the chance to play them for the Final place. They refused, allowing Wales to step in and twice beat Israel 2-0, thus qualifying for the finals.

In their first pool match, Wales played well and drew 1-1 with a dispirited Hungary, John Charles of Juventus scoring their goal. They then put in a mediocre performance against Mexico, again drawing 1-1, and followed this up with a rather dull goalless draw with hosts Sweden, who had already qualified for the next round.

Wales met Brazil in the quarter-finals

Above: *Wales attempt to stop Pelé from scoring for Brazil in 1958*

and, to their eternal credit, held out for 65 minutes, before a shot from Pelé was deflected past 'keeper Kelsey. The Principality has not qualified for the finals of the World Cup since 1958, although they have come close once or twice. Wales' recent success in Rugby Union has not been matched by the football team, but despite this there is continued hope that one day Wales will finally qualify for a World Cup tournament.

Wembley

Originally known as the Empire Stadium, Wembley was constructed in 300 days at a cost of £750,000 as the centrepiece of the Empire Exhibition. The stadium's first event, the FA Cup Final on 28 April 1923, was nearly abandoned because of congestion caused by the FA's pay-at-the-gate policy. The day was famously saved by Constable George Scorey and his white horse Billy who controlled a crowd which official figures put at 125,000 but was rumoured to be as high as 200,000. After a delayed start Bolton beat West Ham 2-0.

The first of 224 England matches to be played at Wembley was the Home International against Scotland on 12 April 1924, a 2-2 draw in front of 37,250. For many years, Wembley tended to be reserved for showpiece occasions like the Cup Final and the hotly contested home international between England and Scotland. In May 1951 the stadium hosted its first friendly international when England beat Argentina 2-1 but it was not until May 1957 that a World

Cup qualifying game was held there, a 5-1 victory over the Republic of Ireland. In the meantime, Hungary humbled England 6-3 in 1953, becoming the first overseas team to win on English soil.

A two-year programme of refurbishment began in 1961, the first major changes to the stadium, apart from the installation of floodlights in 1953. The new look Wembley's 100,000 capacity comprised 45,000 seats and standing for 55,000. The translucent roof provided shelter for all; previously only 22,000 were under cover.

The stadium's finest hour was the 1966 World Cup Final, held on 30 July. Wembley had played host to all but one of the Group A games and all England's matches in the tournament. The late switch of semi-final venue from Goodison Park provoked some controversy, particularly opponents Portugal. After 1966, all England's home games were played at Wembley until its closure in 2000.

Following the Hillsborough Disaster in 1989, Wembley, like all English stadia, was required to convert to all-seater. In the process, its capacity was reduced to 80,000.

Euro '96 became the stadium's second

major football tournament and later that year Wembley won a competition to site a new national stadium. The last game in front of the Twin Towers, in October 2000, was an inauspicious affair with England losing a World Cup qualifier 1-0 to Germany, prompting manager Kevin Keegan to resign immediately afterwards. Thereafter, England internationals rotated round the country's major club grounds. The new stadium with its distinctive arch was finally opened in 2007 after many delays and is now known as 'The New Wembley' by many fans.

Above: *An internal view of the new Wembley Stadium*

World Cup Willie

The First mascot at FIFA's showcase tournament was 'World Cup Willie' – a football-playing lion – in 1966. The cartoon character was used to help promote the event and was even the subject of the official song. Since then various cartoon mascots have been introduced offering a flavour of the host nation. 'Juanito', a Mexican boy, arrived in 1970 and both West Germany with 'Tip and Tap' in 1974 and Argentina with 'Gauchito' in 1978 continued the young footballers theme. Spain (1982) went for 'Naranjito', an orange, while Mexico (1986) came up with 'Pique', a chilli pepper. Italy's 'Ciao' in 1990 was a stick-figure player and the United States gave us 'Striker', a smiling dog in 1994. France crowed about their cockerel 'Footix' – and their team – in 1998, then four years later Korea and Japan presented 'Kaz, Ato and Nik'. These three computer-generated creatures, collectively known as 'The Spheriks', lived in a place called Atmozone high in the sky and the organisers hoped they would enhance the unique World Cup atmosphere. The trio proved forgettable, however, and for 2006 Germany turned to the US-based Jim Henson Company, producers of The Muppets. They unveiled 'Goleo VI', a human-sized lion puppet, and sidekick 'Pille', a talking football with an encyclopaedic knowledge of the game. South Africa produced Zakumi, a leopard, as their 2010 mascot. The three-banded armadillo mascot for the 2014 Finals was named 'Fuleco'.

X-rated Tackles

In 1998, FIFA announced that tackles from behind would be automatically punished with a red card – a move designed to offer more protection to attackers. How Ferenc Puskas, for one, would have loved that sort of protection. In 1954, the legendary Hungarian was effectively kicked out of the competition by German centre-half Werner Liebrich. In 1966 Pelé faced some dreadful Portuguese tackles, topped by a brutal double foul by João Morais – who was allowed to stay on the field, while Pelé limped out of the tournament.

Portugal were villains again in 2002, showing their ill-discipline against South Korea. João Pinto's nasty airborne, two-footed lunge from behind on Park Ji-Sung was 'rewarded' with a red card. Italian Mario David's karate kick to the neck of Leonel Sanchez of Chile also led to a sending-off. The violent, X-rated 1962 clash was tagged 'The Battle of Santiago'. Twenty years later West German goalkeeper Harald Schumacher's vicious forearm smash to the face of Frenchman Patrick Battiston incredibly went unpunished.

Benjamin Massing of Cameroon received his just desserts in 1990, though. Argentinean winger Claudio Caniggia set off on an upfield foray. He rode two wild tackles but couldn't escape Massing, who launched a waist high, horizontal flying body check. The assault has since been described thus: 'The intent seemed not to be so much to break Caniggia's legs but more to separate them from the rest of his body.'

X-tra Time

The energy-sapping nature of extra time has stressed fans the world over. The 1970 semi-final between Italy and West Germany finished 1-1 after 90 minutes, but five goals flew in during the extra half-hour as the game seesawed wonderfully. The Germans levelled at 3-3 with ten minutes remaining, only for Gianni Rivera to promptly put Italy 4-3 up with the crucial strike.

The first instance of extra time came in 1934. Austria and France scored a goal apiece in the first round encounter before Austria's Anton Scall scored the first World Cup extra-time goal as his side ran out 3-2 victors. Host nation Italy won the 1934 tournament, coming back from a goal behind to beat Czechoslovakia 2-1 after extra time. And it was another host nation, England, who kept their nerve in 1966. Manager Alf Ramsey rallied his troops after West Germany had levelled at 2-2 in the closing stages of normal time. Geoff Hurst's controversial strike restored England's lead and he wrapped things up with his hat-trick goal.

France's Laurent Blanc scored the first extra time 'golden goal', in the

113th minute of a second-round match with Paraguay in 1998. French referee Michel Vautrot was obviously absorbed in the 1990 semi-final between Italy and Argentina – he added eight minutes to the first half of the extra period, later admitting he simply forgot the time!

Xuereb

When French striker Daniel Xuereb came on as a substitute for Bruno Bellone in the World Cup semi-final against West Germany in 1986, he filled in a gap between Julio Abbadie of Uruguay and Spain's Andoni Zubizarreta. Xuereb's arrival on the pitch – for the Final 24 minutes of France's 2-0 defeat – meant that every letter in the alphabet had been used for players' surnames since the start of the Championships in 1930.

That first Final set the alphabetic trend by serving up, amongst others, players whose surnames started with the letters A to G: Andrade, Ballesteros, Castro, Dorado (all Uruguay), Evaristo (Argentina), Fernandez (Uruguay) and Gestido (Uruguay).

The longest surname of a player at World Cup finals was, wait for it, Lefter Kucukandonyadis, who played for Turkey in the 1954 finals, long before surnames were included on the reverse of a player's shirt.

Jan Vennegoor of Hesselink, meanwhile, made a brief cameo at the 2006 Finals.

Above: Xuereb of France in action for Montpellier

Yashin

Below: *Portugal's
Eusebio puts his
penalty kick past
Lev Yashin, in
1966*

Lev Yashin was probably the greatest goalkeeper of all time. Born in 1929, he featured in three World Cups, played for Dinamo Moscow for 22 seasons and set the standards for other keepers to follow. He had total command of his area, was a great shot-stopper and had remarkable positional sense. He would use all legal means at his disposal to prevent the ball from entering the net, and would often kick the ball away when keepers of lesser talent would have attempted to grab it. He was also a wonderful saver of penalties. Known as the Black Panther, because he always wore black, Yashin was the Soviet Union's first choice goalkeeper from 1954 until 1967. He played in the 1958, 1962 and 1966 finals – and was largely responsible for the Soviets getting as far as the semi-finals in 1966. In 1963 he was voted European Footballer of the Year, the first goalkeeper to be awarded the honour.

Yashin continued to play until the age of 41 years, but life was not kind to him after that. In 1986 he lost a leg following a knee operation and four years later, following more surgical complications, he died at the age of 61.

Yugoslavia

The former Yugoslavia used to mix it with the very best on the world football scene. They were runners–up in the European Championships in 1960 and 1968 and won the Olympic Games football tournament in 1960 and were silver medallists in 1948, 1952 and 1956. With that kind of pedigree Yugoslavia were considered dark horses at many World Cup finals. They reached the semi-finals in 1930 and 1962 and as recently as 1990, when they only lost out at the quarter-final stage on penalties to Argentina after a 0-0 draw. Back in 1930, it was a case of 'if only'. Seculic gave Yugoslavia the lead in the fourth minute of their semi-final against Uruguay, only for the Uruguayans to respond with two goals before halftime. Yugoslavia were denied an equaliser by a controversial offside decision and were then over-run by the eventual champions in the second half, losing 6-1.

Over the years Dragan Dzajic played a record 85 games for the country, while top international scorer was Stjepan Bobek with 38 goals. These records are now set in stone since the former Yugoslavia is now divided into separate countries: Croatia, Slovenia, Bosnia-Herzegovena and FYR Macedonia. What remained of the once-great footballing nation of Yugoslavia was officially renamed Serbia and Montenegro in 2003.

Above: Predrag Mijatovic goes in on Andreas Kopke of Germany during the 1998 World Cup

Zagalo

One of only two men (Germany's Franz Beckenbauer is the other) to have won the World Cup as both a player and a manager, Mario Zagallo was born on 9 August 1931 and played on the left wing in the triumphant Brazilian sides of 1958 and 1962, scoring one of the goals in the 5-2 win over Sweden in 1958.

It was probably as coach of the 1970 side that he made his mark, taking over from Joao Saldanha and, with a mixture of luck and judgement, came up with a team that could and did beat the best in the world. He restored Pelé to the side (unthinkable that anyone could have dropped him from the Brazil side, but Saldanha did just that), put Rivelino on the left wing, which brought the best out of Gerson and created space for a recovered Tostao (he had been out of the game amid fears for his sight after a

detached retina) and watched, along with the rest of the world, as Brazil swept all before them in 1970, culminating in a 4-1 win over Italy in the Final.

Later, spells as his country's technical director saw him involved when Brazil won the Cup for a fourth time in 1994 (against Italy, this time on penalties), but four years later was held to blame for Brazil's defeat in the Final against France. Zagallo was placed in a no-win situation however, for he had originally drawn up a team sheet for the Final that omitted Ronaldo, suffering from a mystery illness, from the line-up. There is still speculation, never confirmed, that sponsors forced Ronaldo's reinstatement into the side, but he was obviously below par on the day and Brazil slipped to defeat. Zagallo's luck, at its highest in 1970, deserted him in 1998.

Zenga

Born in Milan in 1960, Walter Zenga had ambitions of following in the footsteps of Dino Zoff and began his playing career with the likes of Salernitana, Savona and Sambenedettese before a switch to Inter Milan in 1982. That of course was the year that Zoff captained Italy to World Cup triumph.

After being reserve at the 1986 tournament Walter became first choice in time for the 1990 tournament. As hosts, Italy were widely held to be favourites, but a penalty shoot-out defeat by Argentina in the semi-final meant Zenga's hope of emulating Zoff came to an end, Italy finishing third. By the time the 1994 tournament came around, Zenga was no longer a member of the squad (he had won a total of 58 caps) and had also switched clubs, moving on to Sampdoria. He spent two years there before moving on to Padova and subsequently to the US to join the New England Revolution. His playing career effectively came to an end in 1999, although he officially remained player-coach at the New England

Left: Walter Zenga tries to save a header from Claudio Caniggia of Argentina in the World Cup semi-final, 1990

Revolution. Since 1998 he has coached 13 club sides and in 2013 was coaching his third UAE team.

Zico

Oone of the most gifted footballers to ever play for Brazil, Zico must consider himself unlucky to have only won a bronze medal with the four times World Champions. Born Artur Antunes Coimbra in Rio in 1953, he was the youngest of five footballing brothers. Already the South American Player of the Year in 1977, his 1978 World Cup campaign was blighted by injuries and dissatisfaction with the manager's defensive tactics. In Spain four years later, a more attacking Brazil entertained the crowds. Four goals in tally past the half-century but he was unable to inspire his country past the second phase.

Although they emerged victorious in an all-South American clash with Argentina, the Brazilians could not prevent eventual winners Italy from halting their campaign. Three substitute appearances followed for Zico in 1986, including one in the quarter-final against France when he missed a penalty minutes after the crowd's chanting had persuaded coach Tele Santana to introduce him into the action. He made amends in the penalty shootout that followed, but misses from Socrates and Julio Cesar meant that Zico's World Cup dream was over. He followed retirement by being appointed Brazil's Sports Minister before coaching spells with Japan, Iraq and a host of club sides in the noughties.

Zidane

French midfield maestro Zinedine Zidane made a sensational impact on his international debut, scoring twice in the closing stages to rescue a 2-2 draw with the Czech Republic in 1994. But it was another brace of goals four years later that ensured he was a household name. Two near-identical flashing headers against Brazil gave France, the hosts, a commanding halftime lead in the 1998 World Cup Final; a third goal from Petit late on completed the scoring.

Zidane was equally imperious as France triumphed at Euro 2000 and, in 2001, became the most expensive player in football history when Real Madrid paid £46m to Juventus – they were getting the finished article and 'Zizou' lead Real to the Champions League title scoring a spectacular winning goal in the Final. At the 2002 World Cup Zidane was struggling with injury and it was no real surprise that France's hopes limped off with him as they were eliminated early on. Zidane was a master of the football, with no end of tricks up his sleeve, but the key to his iconic status – like all truly great players – was a fierce work-rate and the ability of

Above: Zidane scores for France in the World Cup Final of 1998 and then duly celebrates

knowing when to play it simple and when to pull off something extraordinary.

He was named FIFA Player of the Year in 1998 and retired after the much-publicised sending off (for a head-butt) during the 2006 Final against Italy.

Right: *Zoff prepares to take a goal-kick during the 1982 World Cup in Spain*

Below: *Zoff carrying the World Cup after defeating West Germany in 1982*

Zoff

Italian Dino Zoff is not only one of the best goalkeepers the world has ever seen, he's an extraordinary record-breaker, too.

Zoff made his World Cup finals bow in 1974 in West Germany where Italy were unexpectedly eliminated at the group stage. By that time, however, he had set an international record of 1143 minutes without conceding. Haiti's goal in Italy's 3-1 opening group match halting that wonderful run. His most cherished prize came eight years later in Spain. After a slow start – the Italians only managed three draws against Poland, Peru and Cameroon in the group – Zoff led his side to wins over Argentina, Brazil and Poland leaving them to face West Germany in the Final. At the age of 40 Zoff captained Italy to a 3-1 triumph. It was the 106th of his eventual 112 caps – another record until surpassed by Maldini – and

when he lifted the trophy he became the oldest World Cup winner.

After a domestic playing career with Udinese, Mantova, Napoli and Juventus Zoff turned to coaching with Juventus, Lazio and then the Italian national side. He took Italy to the Final of Euro 2000, but stepped down after they lost to France.

Zubizarreta

One of an elite few who have graced four World Cups, goalkeeper Andoni Zubizarreta made his international debut against Finland in 1985. Born in Vitoria Spain in 1961, Zubi went on to win 126 caps for his country before his retirement in 1998. His World Cup career got off to an inauspicious start with a 1-0 defeat at the hands of Brazil. Victories followed against Northern Ireland, Algeria and Denmark before a quarter-final tie with Belgium saw Zubizarreta truly earning his wages in a penalty shoot-out which the Spanish lost 5-4.

Italia '90 saw Zubi keep a clean sheet in Spain's opening match against Uruguay but he could not prevent them going out in the second round to Yugoslavia. Four years later in America, he experienced another quarter-final defeat, this time at the hands of a Roberto Baggio-inspired Italy while in 1998 he pushed the ball into his own net for one of Nigeria's goals in Spain's opening defeat that, coupled with a 0-0 draw against Paraguay, saw them fail to progress past the first round. Zubizarreta finished his domestic career having played more than 600 League games, winning six League titles and three Cups, along with European Cup Winners' Cup and Champions' League medals.

ALSO AVAILABLE

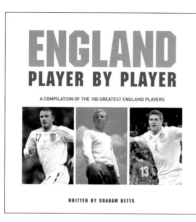

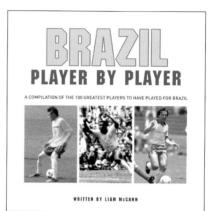

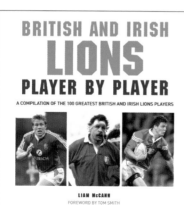

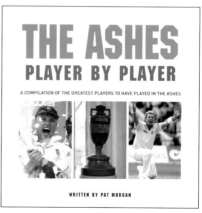

ALSO AVAILABLE

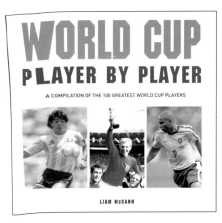

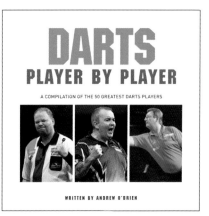

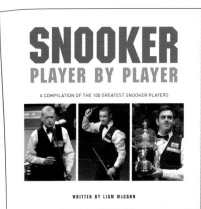

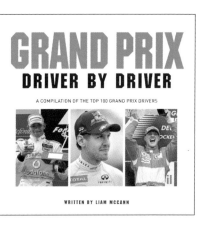

**The pictures in this book were provided
courtesy of the following:**

GETTY IMAGES
101 Bayham Street, London NW1 0AG

EMPICS
www.empics.com

WIKICOMMONS
commons.wikimedia.org

Design & Artwork by Scott Giarnese

Published by G2 Entertainment Limited

Publishers: Jules Gammond & Edward Adams

Written by Michael Heatley with Graham Betts, Mike Gent,
David Lloyd, Chris Mason, Rod Gilmour and Jules Gammond